Instant BIBLE LESSONS For PRETEENS

Our Awesome God

Mary J. Davis

For information regarding the CPSIA on this printed material call:
203-595-3636 and provide reference # LANC-538867

rainbowpublishers®

Rainbow Publishers • P.O. Box 261129 • San Diego, CA 92196
www.RainbowPublishers.com

To my preteen inspirations: Shelbee, Michael, Brandon, and Vincent.
To my inspiration in all I do: Larry, our children, and our eight beautiful grandchildren.

INSTANT BIBLE LESSONS FOR PRETEENS: OUR AWESOME GOD
©2014 by Rainbow Publishers, seventh printing
ISBN 10: 1-58411-075-9
ISBN 13: 978-1-58411-075-0
Rainbow reorder# RB38612
RELIGION / Christian Ministry / Youth

Rainbow Publishers
P.O. Box 261129
San Diego, CA 92196
www.RainbowPublishers.com

SUSTAINABLE FORESTRY INITIATIVE

Certified Sourcing
www.sfiprogram.org
SFI-00484

Cover Illustrator: Jennifer Kalis
Interior Illustrator: Apryl Stott

Scriptures are from the *Holy Bible: New International Version* (North American Edition),
©1973, 1978, 1984 by the International Bible Society. Used by permission of Zondervan Bible Publishers.

Printed in the United States of America

Contents

Introduction

Let's face it: the preteen years are a struggle. Bodily changes, emotional highs and lows, and hormones run amok are just some of the challenges of this age. The world bombards our preteens with unsavory messages at every turn. They need encouragement and opportunity to put God's Word into their hearts and minds. The best tools we can give our preteens to survive in the world today are God's Holy Word and our guidance. In *Our Awesome God*, preteens will learn that our God is a loving God who expects obedience. He is willing and able to help us throughout life's wilderness paths. God is indeed AWESOME.

Each of the first eight chapters includes a Bible story, memory verse, alternative forms of learning the lesson theme, and a variety of activities to help reinforce the truth in the lesson. An additional chapter contains miscellaneous projects that can be used anytime throughout the study, or at the end to review the lessons.

The most exciting aspect of *Instant Bible Lessons for Preteens* is its flexibility. You can easily adapt these lessons to a Sunday school hour, a children's church service, a Wednesday night Bible study, or family home use. Because there is a variety of reproducible ideas from which to choose, you will enjoy creating a class session that is best for your group of students, whether large or small, beginning or advanced, active or studious, all boys/all girls/co-ed. The intriguing topics will keep your students coming back for more, week after week.

✳ How to Use This Book ✳

Each chapter begins with a Bible story. You may simply tell the story from the story page, or use the first activity to discover the lesson in a more involved way. To prepare for each lesson, duplicate the story page. Read the Bible Scriptures and the story written on the page to get a good background of the lesson you will teach your students. Jot down any thoughts that will help you teach the Bible story. Use the discussion questions to spark conversation about the Bible story.

| bulletin board | craft | express yourself | game | group |

| song | puzzle | skit | teacher help | think |

CHAPTER 1

Our Awesome God Guides His Creation

MEMORY VERSE

As long as the earth endures, seedtime and harvest, cold and heat, summer and winter, day and night will never cease.
GENESIS 8:22

* The Big Boat *

God created a beautiful earth with plants, animals, and people. Before long, God saw that the people were full of sin and had only evil in their hearts.

This grieved God greatly. So He decided to rid His wonderful earth of all this wickedness. He would use His power as creator and controller of the world to cleanse the earth.

But before God brought about this change, He talked to Noah, a man who loved God and followed His ways. God told Noah to build an ark. He didn't just say, "Build something you think might withstand a great flood." God gave Noah very detailed instructions for building it. Noah spent many years building the ark, just as God instructed.

Then Noah followed God's instructions and filled the ark with two of every creature. Noah also stored plenty of food for the animals and his family.

After all the animals and Noah's family were on the ark, God shut the door. Then the rain started.

It rained for 40 days and nights, causing a great flood. All people and animals were destroyed. Yet the ark floated safely above all the destruction. God kept the animals and Noah's family safe.

The flooding continued for 150 days. Then God caused the water to recede.

Noah sent a dove to see if it was safe to leave the ark. The dove found no place to land because water still covered the earth so the dove returned to the ark. But when Noah sent out the dove again seven days later, it did not return.

God said to Noah, "Come out of the ark." Noah, his family, and all the animals and creatures came out of the ark. The ground was dry, and everything was safe.

Noah built an altar to the Lord to thank Him.

God promised that He never again would end all life with a flood. To show His promise for all generations, God put a rainbow in the sky. When we see a rainbow today, we can remember that God still keeps His promises. God is in control of His world.

BASED ON GENESIS 6:5-9:19

? Discussion Questions

1. Why do you think God wanted to start over by causing the flood to take away all the sinful people?

2. How does God show His power over the earth today?

WHAT YOU NEED

- pages 8 and 9, duplicated
- pencils
- craft sticks

WHAT TO DO

1. Lead the students in discussion as they read and complete the worksheets.
2. Allow time for questions and further discussion so the students fully understand the pain, plan, protection, and promise of God throughout the timeline of the flood.

* The Four P's *

1. God's Pain - Genesis 6:6-7

What one word appears in both of these verses that tells us God was sorry He had created man?

— — — — — — —

What does Genesis 6:5 tell us about why God felt this way?
Think about your own life. What things might you do today to cause God to feel this way?

2. God's Plan - Genesis 6:9-22

Finish the three words from Genesis 6:9 that describe Noah:

R__ __ __ __ __ __ __
B__ __ __ __ __ __ __ __
W__ __ __ __ __ with God

Why do you think God gave Noah exact instructions on how to build the ark? What do you think would happen if you were asked to use craft sticks and glue to build an ark without instructions? Do you think each ark would look the same?
Have you or your parents tried to put together something you bought without reading the instructions? What happened? Write or tell about someone you know who tried to assemble or cook something without following the instructions.

Think about it
God gave Noah exact instructions because He knew which type of wood would withstand the

flood waters. He knew the ark had to be coated in pitch. He knew how much room would be needed to hold all the animals, Noah's family, and food for the journey.

Point to Remember
Our awesome God gave Noah the exact instructions he needed to save his family and the animals that would replenish the earth.

3. God's Protection - Genesis 7:11–8:19

Read Genesis 7:17-24. What do you think it felt like to be in that rocking ark for a long time? Have you ridden on a roller coaster or other moving ride that nearly made you sick? How would you handle that same motion for 150 days?

Point to Remember
Write the first four words of Genesis 8:1. Throughout all the flooding, destruction, and destroying of every other living thing on earth, our awesome God protected Noah, his family, and every creature inside the ark.

4. God's Promise - Genesis 8:20–9:17

Read Genesis 8:20. What was the first thing Noah did after everyone and every creature came out of the ark?

Read Genesis 9:8-17. What sign did God use to remind all generations of His promise to never send a flood to destroy the entire earth again?

Do you think God expected the world to be perfect and free from sin forever, even after the flood?

Point to Remember
Our Awesome God gave His promise to all generations. No matter how wicked the world seems, God has promised not to destroy it with a great flood.

Summary
Our Awesome God controls the world He created. How does it make you feel to know that the same God who sent a flood to destroy all evil in the world loves you very much? What does it mean to you that God controls the world He created?

Think Deeper
1. If God controls the world He created, how did humankind become so evil and wicked? Could God have made people into beings who would only obey Him and not sin? Why do you think He did not do that?

2. God briefly got rid of wickedness with the great flood. What larger plan had God already decided on to save us from our sins?

* Memory Verse * Thermometer

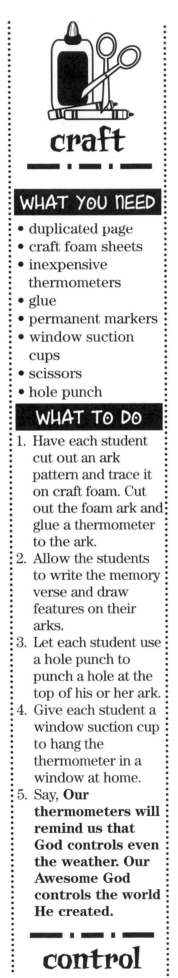

craft

WHAT YOU NEED

- duplicated page
- craft foam sheets
- inexpensive thermometers
- glue
- permanent markers
- window suction cups
- scissors
- hole punch

WHAT TO DO

1. Have each student cut out an ark pattern and trace it on craft foam. Cut out the foam ark and glue a thermometer to the ark.
2. Allow the students to write the memory verse and draw features on their arks.
3. Let each student use a hole punch to punch a hole at the top of his or her ark.
4. Give each student a window suction cup to hang the thermometer in a window at home.
5. Say, **Our thermometers will remind us that God controls even the weather. Our Awesome God controls the world He created.**

control

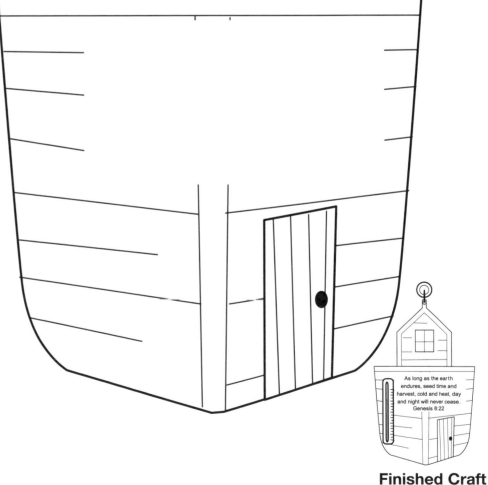

As long as the earth endures, seed time and harvest, cold and heat, day and night will never cease.
Genesis 8:22

Finished Craft

✴ Search the Word ✴

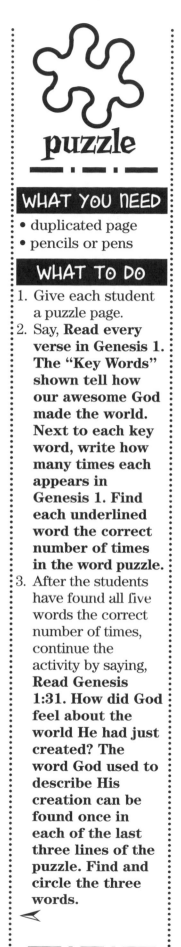

Key Words

created	____
made	____
said	____
called	____
blessed	____

```
d o g s c t r e e m a d e s k i e s
a n i m a l r b i r d s i m a g e s
n o o d l e s e c r e a t e d r e d
d i g g i n g x a o x i c a n i d x
e e l s b n a d l t o d o a b o a x
l a v a l a m p l l e d i d l p x m s
i d l e e d l i e h m c r a e l o x
o n l y s a i d d i a s t o s l e t
n o s e s y e k n o d c a t s g o d
s e a t e d d e t a e r c p e t s i
c a r e d a m x c r e a t e d x x a
l e o p a r d s a i d s h e e p q s
u n i v e r s e l e v e l s t a r s
m o n k e y s a l l s l e e p n o w
r h i n o m a d e t a l l s o u p s
h e n s c h i x d i c g i r a f f e
c r e a t e d g o o d g r i e v e d
l i v i n g x g r i e v e d g o o d
b n k d i a s g r i e v e d d o o g
```

puzzle

WHAT YOU NEED
- duplicated page
- pencils or pens

WHAT TO DO

1. Give each student a puzzle page.
2. Say, **Read every verse in Genesis 1. The "Key Words" shown tell how our awesome God made the world. Next to each key word, write how many times each appears in Genesis 1. Find each underlined word the correct number of times in the word puzzle.**
3. After the students have found all five words the correct number of times, continue the activity by saying, **Read Genesis 1:31. How did God feel about the world He had just created? The word God used to describe His creation can be found once in each of the last three lines of the puzzle. Find and circle the three words.**

WHAT TO DO, CONTINUED

➤ 4. Say, **Read Genesis 6:5-6. How did God feel about the world He had created after people became full of sin?** [grieved] **This word has seven letters and can be found once in each of the last three lines of the puzzle. Find and circle the three words.**

control

craft

WHAT YOU NEED

- pages 12 and 13, duplicated
- cardboard (2 feet square)
- cardboard gift
- wrap tubes, six
- trash bags 30-33 gallon size, 3
- old newspapers
- duct tape
- scissors
- rulers
- pencils

WHAT TO DO

1. Divide the class into two teams.
2. Place the items for each project on a table. Have each team work in a different spot to allow plenty of room to move around.
3. After the projects are finished, say, **Isn't it wonderful to have a God who controls the world He created? Only God could have given Noah the exact instructions he needed to build the ark, and gather and care for the animals.**

control

∗ Befuddled Blueprints ∗

Materials list for Project 1
- cardboard (2 feet x 2 feet)
- 6 gift wrap tubes
- pencils
- duct tape
- scissors
- ruler or measuring tape

Project 1 instructions

1. Place cardboard on floor or a table.
2. Measure out a square exactly 2 feet along each side. Mark the square with a pencil.
3. Cut out the square.
4. Measure 15 inches from one end of a cardboard tube.
5. Cut the tube at 15 inches. Repeat with a second tube.
6. Measure 2 feet from one end of one cardboard tube.
7. Cut the tube at two feet. Repeat with a second tube.
8. Measure a spot 3 inches in from each corner of the flat cardboard piece. Number the corners from 1 to 4.
9. Use duct tape to fasten one end of one of the 15-inch cardboard tubes to the number 1 spot marked on a corner of the flat cardboard piece.
10. Use duct tape to fasten the other 15-inch cardboard tube piece to the number 3 spot on the flat cardboard piece.
11. Use duct tape to fasten one 2-foot length of the cardboard tube to spot number 2 on the flat cardboard piece.
12. Use duct tape to fasten the second 2-foot length to spot number 4 on the flat cardboard piece.
13. Turn the object upside down, so that it rests on the cardboard tubes.
14. Oops…now you must measure and cut 9 inches from each of the two longer cardboard tube pieces.
15. Now you're finished. If you have two leftover cardboard tubes, and the object sits evenly on the floor without wobbling, you've finished your project.

What is it?

Materials list for Project 2

- three large trash bags, 30-33 gallon size
- old newspapers
- ruler or measuring tape
- scissors
- duct tape

Project 2 instructions

1. Spread newspapers on a table. Put the papers in piles of at least five sheets each.

2. Use a ruler and pencil to mark a 12-inch square. Cut out the pile of 12-inch squares.

3. Use a ruler and pencil to mark a 10-inch square. Cut out the pile of 10-inch squares.

4. Use a ruler and pencil to mark an 8-inch square. Cut out the pile of 8-inch squares.

5. Open the trash bag. Wad up all the scrap newspapers, one sheet at a time, and stuff each sheet into the trash bag. Push the papers tightly into the bag so you can fit all the scraps inside one bag.

6. If the bag tears, remove all the papers and put them inside a fresh trash bag.

7. Fold all the 12-inch squares in half, then in half the other way. This will make several 6-inch folded squares. Lay these aside for now.

8. Fold all the 10-inch squares in half, to make 5" x 10" pieces of folded paper. Lay these aside for now.

9. Fold all the 8-inch squares in half, then in half again…well, no, just wad them up and add them to the trash bag.

10. Gather the opened edge of the trash bag and twist until the bag is tightly closed. Use duct tape to hold the bag closed.

11. Use duct tape to fasten all the leftover folded pieces of paper to the outside of the trash bag, in random order.

12. Now your project is finished. Have someone sit on the project.

What is it?

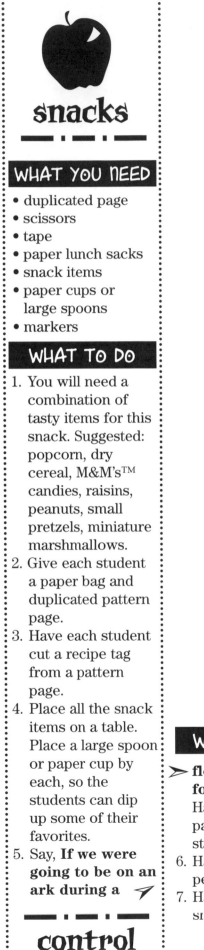

* Long-lasting * Energy Snacks

Longlasting Energy Snacks

_____

_____

_____

_____

_____

_____

_____

_____

_____

_____

WHAT YOU NEED

- duplicated page
- scissors
- tape
- paper lunch sacks
- snack items
- paper cups or large spoons
- markers

WHAT TO DO

1. You will need a combination of tasty items for this snack. Suggested: popcorn, dry cereal, M&M's™ candies, raisins, peanuts, small pretzels, miniature marshmallows.
2. Give each student a paper bag and duplicated pattern page.
3. Have each student cut a recipe tag from a pattern page.
4. Place all the snack items on a table. Place a large spoon or paper cup by each, so the students can dip up some of their favorites.
5. Say, **If we were going to be on an ark during a**

WHAT TO DO, CONTINUED

➤ **flood for at least 150 days, we would need some high-energy food. Let's make a snack mix using our favorite snack items.** Have the students dip some of the items of their choice into their paper bags. They should fill their bags about halfway. Have the students shake up their snack bags to mix the items inside.

6. Have the students use markers to write their "ingredients" for a perfect energy snack on their paper recipe tags.
7. Have the students tape the recipe tags onto the fronts of their snack bags.

* God's Promise *
Spinners

Genesis 8:22

bulletin board

WHAT YOU NEED

- duplicated page
- junk mail CDs
- plastic lids or paper plates
- glue
- scissors
- fishing line
- markers
- tape

WHAT TO DO

1. Give each student a pattern page and a CD.
2. Have the students cut the figures from the pattern pages. Allow them to decorate each pattern.
3. Instruct the students to glue the paper figures onto the CDs.
4. Show how to tape a length of fishing line to the top of each finished project. Hang the spinners in your classroom.
5. Say, **The rainbow reminds us of the promise God made when He placed the rainbow in the sky for the first**

control

WHAT TO DO, CONTINUED

➤ time. Who can tell us what that promise is? Our memory verse from Genesis 8:22 reminds us that our Awesome God controls the world He created.

* God is in Control *

WHAT YOU NEED
- duplicated page
- pens or pencils

WHAT TO DO

1. Give each student a duplicated page.
2. Allow time for the students to express their feelings about God.
3. Remind the students that God lovingly created the entire universe, including human beings. God destroyed the creatures on the earth, but not the entire earth. He saved the earth to renew itself through new growth. He saved Noah's family and two of each creature to begin a new world. God is the God of creation, and the God of new beginnings.

Our awesome God controls the world He created. The great flood is only one example from the Bible that proves God's control over His creation. Use the space below to express yourself and tell how you feel knowing that God is in control of everything. When your life seems to be out of control, how do you feel about having an awesome and loving God who controls absolutely everything? Write a poem, song, journal entry, or prayer to express your gratitude to your awesome God.

_____

_____

_____

_____

_____

_____

_____

_____

_____

_____

_____

_____

_____

_____

_____

_____

CHAPTER 2

God Leads His People

MEMORY VERSE

You yourselves have seen what I did to Egypt, and how I carried you on eagles' wings and brought you to myself.
EXODUS 19:4

✳ Out of Egypt ✳

The Bible contains many examples of how God leads His people. The longest and most dramatic journey was when God led the Israelites. We can learn about God and how He wants us to live by looking at the Israelites' journey.

God instructed Moses and Aaron to lead the Israelites out of Egypt where they had lived in slavery for 430 years. After suffering through the ten plagues, Pharaoh let the Israelites leave Egypt. God led His people with a floating cloud by day and floating fire by night.

But as soon as his slaves were gone, Pharaoh decided he wanted them back. So he sent his army to recapture the Israelites. The Israelites were soon cornered between the Red Sea and the Egyptian army.

"Why did God lead us out of Egypt just to cause us to be killed by the Egyptians?" the Israelites grumbled.

But God was still leading His people. He parted the Red Sea and dried the ground so the Israelites could cross over safely. Then just as the Egyptian army started across the parted sea, God caused the waters to come together and drown them.

Many times during their travels, the Israelites forgot how much God had done for them and they started to complain instead. But each time, God showed His willingness to lead them, keep them safe, and provide everything they needed.

When the Israelites crossed the Shur Desert, they went three days without water. When they found water, they couldn't drink it because it was bitter. They complained, but God still solved the problem by telling Moses to throw a piece of wood in the water. The water became drinkable.

Then the Israelites came to the Sin Desert, and began to grumble again.

"At least we had food to eat when we were slaves," they said. "We should have stayed slaves!"

Once again, God solved the problem. He sent bread in the morning, and meat in the evening.

Eventually, the Israelites reached the land God had promised them. God had led, protected, and provided for them throughout the journey even when times seemed tough. Just think what He can do for you!

BASED ON EXODUS 12:40-42; 13:17-31; 15–17

❓ Discussion Questions

1. The Israelites complained even though they saw God leading them. Why do you think God didn't give up on them?

2. Why is it so easy to complain? What can we do to avoid complaining?

group

WHAT YOU NEED

- pages 19 and 20, duplicated
- cardboard
- scissors
- tissue wrap (red, orange, and yellow)
- cotton balls
- glue
- punch bowl
- flavored drink mix, two packages
- sugar
- water
- cups
- spoon
- ice cubes
- magnet sheets
- permanent markers
- bottled water
- masking tape or duct tape

WHAT TO DO

1. Before class, decide whether you will do this activity in your classroom, throughout the building, or outdoors.
2. Set up the five rest stops with the supplies as listed.

Rest Stop Supplies:

Stop 1
- duplicated cartoon page (page 20)

Stop 2
- pillar shapes cut from cardboard
- glue
- red, orange, and yellow tissue wrap
- cotton or cotton balls

Stop 3
- punch bowl filled with about a gallon of water
- two packages flavored drink mix
- 1½ cups sugar
- spoon
- cups
- ice cubes

Stop 4
- magnet sheets, cut to 3" x 3"
- several permanent markers

Stop 5
- small bottles of water
- several rolls of masking or duct tape

lead

Leading the Wilderness Walk

Begin the activity by telling the students they will be going on a walk around the room (building or outdoors). Have the students carry their Bibles with them.

Stop 1: History

Give each student a duplicated cartoon story. Have the children sit down and read the cartoons. Ask for volunteers to give a recap of why the Israelites were slaves in Egypt. Encourage the students to look in their Bibles for the Scriptures listed on the cartoon page.

Stop 2: Which way now?

Have at least one student open a Bible and read aloud Exodus 13:21-22. Divide the class into two groups. Have one group make a fire pillar by gluing wadded pieces of tissue wrap onto a cardboard pillar. Have the other group make a cloud pillar by gluing cotton onto the other cardboard pillar. Designate students to carry the cloud and fire.

Stop 3: Sweet water

Select a student to read Exodus 15:22-27 aloud. Choose a student to pour the drink mix into the bowl of water. Choose another student to add the sugar to the mixture. Choose another student to stir the mixture. Give each student a paper cup with some ice cubes. Pour some of the sweetened water into each cup so each student can have a drink. While the students are drinking their sweetened water at the rest stop, have someone read the last half of Exodus 15:25 and verses 26-27 again. Choose someone to read verse 24 again. Ask, **What is the difference in the two Scripture passages we just heard?** (The people grumbled when something went wrong. God wanted the people to learn to listen to Him and obey without grumbling.)

Stop 4: Manna and quail

Have the students open their Bibles to Exodus 16. Let willing students take turns reading it aloud. Give each student a piece of magnet sheet. Have the students use permanent markers to write the memory verse on their magnets. They also can draw pictures of manna and quail, or other food. Remind the students that God always provides for our needs..

Stop 5: Water from a rock

Let the students take turns reading Exodus 17:1-7. Give each student a bottle of water. Have the students tear strips of masking tape or duct tape and place the strips onto their water bottles. Let them cover the bottles to look like rocks as time allows. Remind the students that God provided His people with water from an unusual source in order to show His power and His willingness to provide the things we need.

The history of how God's people became slaves in Egypt.

God says that His people will be slaves in a foreign land. (Genesis 15:12-16)

Joseph is sold by his brothers and taken to Egypt. (Genesis 37:3-4, 23-28)

Joseph interprets Pharaoh's dreams and warns of a famine (Genesis 41:1-40)

Pharaoh puts Joseph in charge of Egypt's land. (Genesis 41:41-44)

Joseph's brothers come to Egypt to find food for their family. (Genesis 42:1-2)

Joseph and his family stay in Egypt. (Genesis 50:22-26)

The Israelite nation grows. The Egyptian rulers decide to make them slaves so they cannot take over the Egyptians. (Exodus 1:1-14)

* Grumble Grumble *
Chant

WHAT YOU NEED

• duplicated page

WHAT TO DO

1. Give each student a copy of the page.
2. Have the students read the chant together. If you have a large class, divide the class into groups.

Grumble, grumble
God's people just grumbled all day.
Not enough water, not enough food,
That's all that they could say.

Grumble, grumble
Not a "thank You" He heard.
God's patience must have been wearing out
Each time He heard those grumbling words.

Grumble, grumble
God continued to provide.
He led His people and took care of them
Each day and each night by their side.

Grumble, grumble
What does He hear from you?
Do you thank Him for all He gives
Or just ask more for Him to do?

Grumble, grumble
It has to hurt God's ears
When He takes such good care of us
And grumbling is all He hears!

lead

group

WHAT YOU NEED

- duplicated page
- chalk boards or white boards
- chalk or white board markers

WHAT TO DO

1. Divide the class into two teams. Have someone from each team write the word "wilderness" across the center of the board.
2. Ask the questions from the duplicated sheet. Give one team the opportunity to answer the question first. If that team can't answer correctly, ask the other team the question. Take turns asking each team the question first.
3. Each time a team answers a question correctly, that team can erase one letter of the "wilderness" from the board. If you run out of questions before the game is finished, go back and ask the questions randomly.

lead

* Wilderness Team *

• In what country were the Israelites slaves?

• Whose plan was it for the Egyptians to enslave God's people?

• What body of water did God part so the people could cross on dry ground?

• How many Egyptians made it across the Red Sea while chasing the Israelites?

• What did God place in front of the Israelites to follow by day?

• What gave the Israelites light and guidance at night?

• What did the people do every time something went wrong?

• What was wrong with the water the Israelites found in the desert?

• What did God have Moses throw into the water to make it taste better?

• What kind of meat did God send to feed the grumbling Israelites?

• What did God make appear on the ground each morning to feed His people?

• How did a rock save the lives of the Israelites in the desert?

Eagle Wings Pin

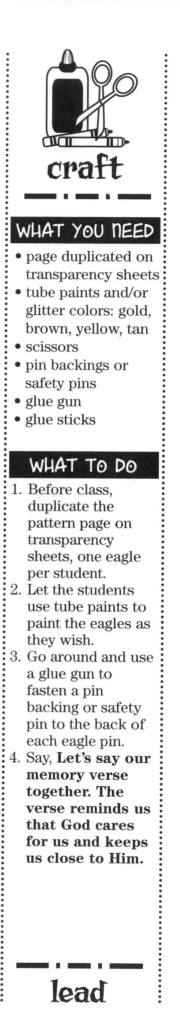

craft

WHAT YOU NEED

- page duplicated on transparency sheets
- tube paints and/or glitter colors: gold, brown, yellow, tan
- scissors
- pin backings or safety pins
- glue gun
- glue sticks

WHAT TO DO

1. Before class, duplicate the pattern page on transparency sheets, one eagle per student.
2. Let the students use tube paints to paint the eagles as they wish.
3. Go around and use a glue gun to fasten a pin backing or safety pin to the back of each eagle pin.
4. Say, **Let's say our memory verse together. The verse reminds us that God cares for us and keeps us close to Him.**

lead

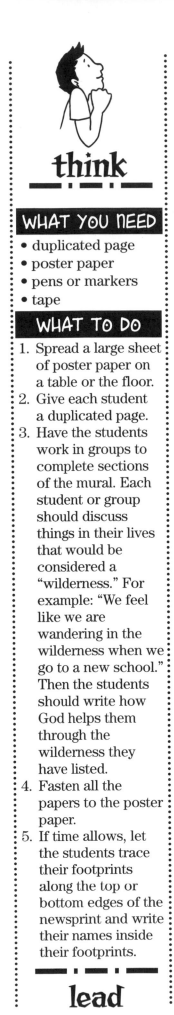

think

WHAT YOU NEED

- duplicated page
- poster paper
- pens or markers
- tape

WHAT TO DO

1. Spread a large sheet of poster paper on a table or the floor.
2. Give each student a duplicated page.
3. Have the students work in groups to complete sections of the mural. Each student or group should discuss things in their lives that would be considered a "wilderness." For example: "We feel like we are wandering in the wilderness when we go to a new school." Then the students should write how God helps them through the wilderness they have listed.
4. Fasten all the papers to the poster paper.
5. If time allows, let the students trace their footprints along the top or bottom edges of the newsprint and write their names inside their footprints.

lead

* Today's * Wilderness Mural

Wilderness

_____
_____
_____
_____
_____
_____
_____
_____

God's Solution

_____
_____
_____
_____
_____
_____
_____
_____

* Papier Mâché Eagle *

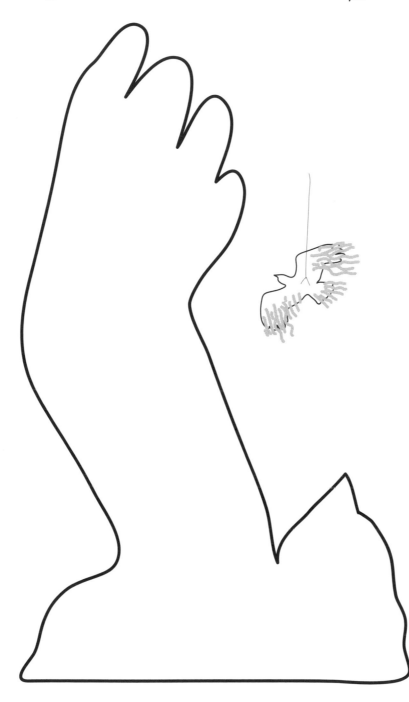

WHAT YOU NEED

- duplicated page
- cardboard
- brown paper grocery bags
- thinned glue
- scissors
- paint and brushes
- black markers
- fishing line
- tape

WHAT TO DO

1. Give each student a pattern page (the pattern is half of the eagle shape).
2. Each student should trace a half-eagle onto cardboard, then turn the pattern over and trace the other half so he or she creates a whole eagle, then cut out the eagle.
3. Have the students cut or tear strips from brown paper bags, then dip the paper strips in the thinned glue. They should cover the tops and bottoms of their eagle shapes with paper strips, shaping the eagles as they go.

WHAT TO DO, CONTINUED

4. Show how to cut some feather-shaped pieces from the brown paper to finish the wing and tail edges.
5. After the eagles have dried, allow the students to paint and decorate the eagles.
6. Have the students write the memory verse on their eagles.
7. Show how to tape loops of fishing line to the tops of the eagles' backs for hangers.

lead

CHAPTER 3

God Makes Us Conquerors

📖 MEMORY VERSE

The Lord said to Joshua, "See, I have delivered Jericho into your hands."
JOSHUA 6:2

✳ Tumbling Walls ✳

Moses had just died, so God made Joshua the leader of His people. God was ready for His people to enter into the land He had promised them. To do so, they had to cross the Jordan River, which God parted for them just as He had parted the Red Sea.

Joshua was to lead an army into battle to win the land that God had promised to them. When Joshua neared Jericho with the army, he looked up and saw a man with a drawn sword in his hand. It was a messenger from the Lord.

"Take off your sandals," the messenger said, "for the place where you are standing is holy."

God told Joshua, "I have delivered Jericho into your hands." Then He gave Joshua specific instructions on how to defeat the army of Jericho. Here is what Joshua was to do:

1. March around the city with the army once a day for six days.
2. Have seven priests carry ram's horns trumpets in front of the ark of the covenant during the march.
3. On the seventh day, march around the city seven times, with the priests blowing the trumpets.
4. Upon hearing a long blast on the trumpets, have all the people give a loud shout.
5. Watch the walls of Jericho collapse, then go straight into the city.

Joshua told the people what God had commanded. They followed God's instructions exactly for six days.

On the seventh day, after the seventh time around the city, the priests sounded the trumpet blast. Joshua told the people, "Shout, for the Lord has given you the city!"

The trumpets blasted, the people shouted, and the walls of the city fell down. Then God's army charged straight in and conquered the city of Jericho, just as God had promised. With God's help, His people were conquerors.

BASED ON JOSHUA 5:13–6:21

❓ Discussion Questions

1. Why do you think God gave such specific instructions to Joshua instead of allowing him just to charge the city with his army in one day?
2. How does God help you conquer difficulties today?

express yourself

WHAT YOU NEED
• duplicated page

WHAT TO DO
1. Give each child a copy of the page with the sign language alphabet.
2. Have the students spell "Jericho" with their hands.
3. Say, **In our memory verse, God tells Joshua that He has delivered Jericho into the hands of Joshua and the army of God. Let's use our hands to spell out the word Jericho. Can you spell out the entire memory verse?**

conquerors

* Speak With * Your Hands

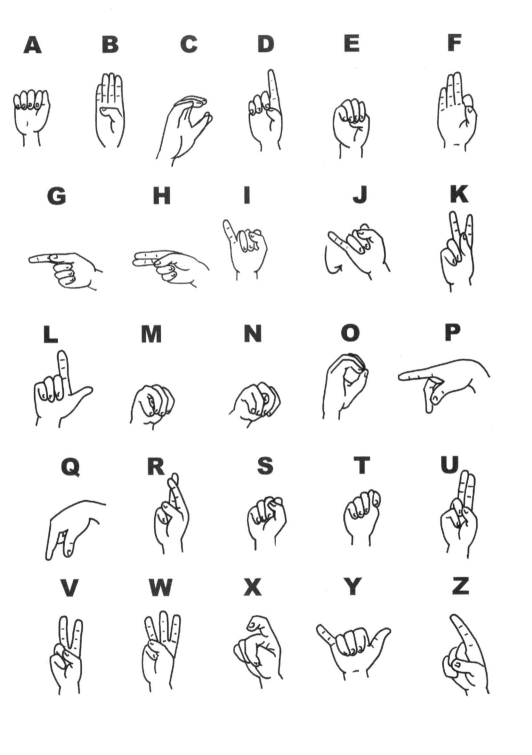

* Acting Out *

group

WHAT TO DO

1. Assign each of seven students one of the paragraphs from the story on page 27, to narrate while the entire class participates in this activity.
2. Give each of seven students a gift wrap tube to use as trumpets.
3. Give each of the remaining students one of the following: two wooden blocks, two pieces of sandpaper, or two plastic lids.
4. In smaller classes, you can have each student do more than one activity.
5. Have the students build a wall with the cardboard boxes and form a large circle around it.
6. Each narrator can step outside the circle when it is his or her turn to narrate.
7. Each time a narrator reads a paragraph, the class should march around the wall once. They should clap blocks together, rub sandpaper together or tap lids together to make the sounds of marching feet. Those carrying trumpets should try to make trumpet sounds with them. Extra narrators should say, "Shhhh" to indicate that the people were not to make a noise except for the marching of their feet and the sounds of the trumpets. The seventh narrator should read the seventh paragraph. The trumpeters should make a long blast, the marching should stop, and all the students should shout. Then the students can knock down the wall and march into the city.

WHAT YOU NEED

- duplicated page
- seven copies of the story on page 27
- wooden blocks
- sandpaper
- plastic lids, any size
- seven gift wrap tubes
- several cardboard boxes, any size

conquerors

✳ Double Puzzle ✳

puzzle

WHAT YOU NEED
- duplicated page
- pencils or pens

WHAT TO DO

1. Give each student a pattern page.
2. Say, **God told Joshua to do something that he had also told Moses to do.**
3. In the first puzzle, unscramble the words to find out what God told Joshua to do. Check your answers in Joshua 5:15. In the second puzzle, four E's are missing. Fill in the E's to find out why God commanded Joshua to do what you discovered in the first puzzle.
4. Ask, **Do you feel that we show reverence to God because He helps us conquer the obstacles in our lives?** Remind the students that there is a difference between trusting God to help us be conquerors, and doing things only so God will help us out of our tough spots.

conquerors

Puzzle 1

___ ___ ___   ___ ___ ___   ___ ___ ___ ___   ___ ___ ___ ___ ___ ___,
k T e a   f o f   u o r y   d n l s s a a,

___ ___ ___   ___ ___ ___   ___ ___ ___ ___ ___   ___ ___ ___ ___
r f o   e t h   c e l a p   e e r h w

___ ___ ___   ___ ___ ___   ___ ___ ___ ___ ___ ___ ___ ___   ___ ___   ___ ___ ___ ___.
o y u   r e a   d n i n g t a d s   s i   l y o h.

Puzzle 2:

R __ V __ R __ N C __

30

* Conquerors * Discussion Starters

1. **Bible:** What do you think would have happened if some of the people had decided to shout on the second march around the walls instead of the seventh?
Today: What happens when you intentionally break a rule at home?

2. **Bible:** How do you think God would have reacted if the army became tired and stopped marching on the third or fourth days?
Today: How does God feel if you decide you are too tired to go to church?

3. **Bible:** How did Joshua's army conquer Jericho?
Today: How do you think we can become conquerors of the obstacles in our own lives?

4. **Bible:** God placed a man with a sword in front of Joshua to give Joshua the instructions for how to conquer Jericho. Who do you think that man was?
Today: How do you think God sends us the message that we can overcome life's obstacles?

Additional questions
- What are some of the obstacles in today's life that we can overcome with God's help?

- What did you learn from the lesson of Joshua and the battle of Jericho?

WHAT YOU NEED
- duplicated page

WHAT TO DO
1. Use the questions to start discussions. There are four sets of questions. Each set has a question about the Bible story, followed by a related question that brings the story into today's world.
2. Allow the students to contribute all they wish to say. Draw some of the quieter students into the discussion.

conquerors

Conquerors Visor

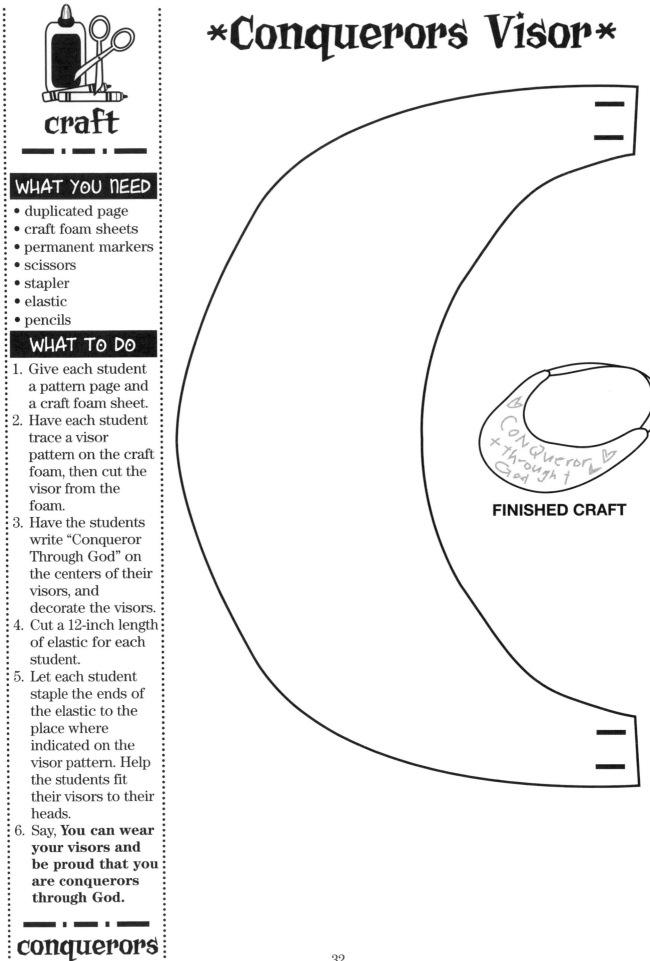

FINISHED CRAFT

craft

WHAT YOU NEED

- duplicated page
- craft foam sheets
- permanent markers
- scissors
- stapler
- elastic
- pencils

WHAT TO DO

1. Give each student a pattern page and a craft foam sheet.
2. Have each student trace a visor pattern on the craft foam, then cut the visor from the foam.
3. Have the students write "Conqueror Through God" on the centers of their visors, and decorate the visors.
4. Cut a 12-inch length of elastic for each student.
5. Let each student staple the ends of the elastic to the place where indicated on the visor pattern. Help the students fit their visors to their heads.
6. Say, **You can wear your visors and be proud that you are conquerors through God.**

conquerors

What Does the
Verse Mean for Me?

Lying (someone has lied to me)	**Lying** (I tell lies)
Gossiping (I like to gossip)	**Gossiping** (others gossip about me)
Fear	**Peer pressure**
Indifference to others	**Disagreements with parents**
Feeling distant from God	**Don't like myself**

WHAT YOU NEED

- duplicated page
- index cards
- glue
- scissors

WHAT TO DO

1. Before class, cut out the situation cards from the pattern page. Glue each card onto an index card.
2. Place all the cards face down on a table.
3. Have the students take turns choosing cards. Each student should read aloud the phrase on the card. The student next to the card-reader should begin the round by naming a godly way to conquer the situation written on the card. Continue around the circle until everyone has had an opportunity to offer a solution.
4. After each round, have the class say the memory verse together, but substitute the

WHAT TO DO, CONTINUED

➤ phrase on the card in place of the word "Jericho" in the memory verse.

5. The person to the left of the card-reader should draw the next card.
6. If your class is large, divide the class into groups and make two or more sets of cards to use.

conquerors

* Acrostic Expression *

WHAT YOU NEED
- duplicated page
- pens or pencils

WHAT TO DO

1. Give each student a duplicated page.
2. Say, **God makes us conquerors. How awesome is that? The word "conqueror" is written on the page. Make an acrostic list, verse, or prayer out of ways God makes you a conqueror.** Suggest: honesty, forgiving, strength, trust, etc.
3. Students may use their pages as journal pages, additions to their bulletin boards at home, or plaques to put up in their rooms at home.

conquerors

C
O
N
Q
U
E
R
O
R

✳ Memory Verse Brick ✳

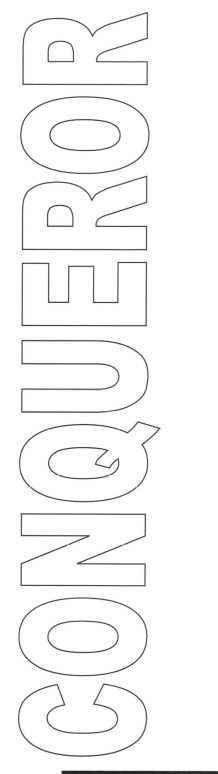

CONQUEROR

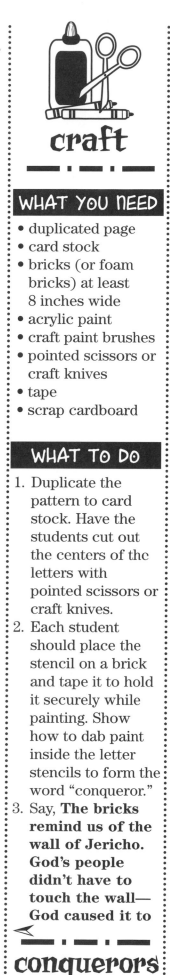

craft

WHAT YOU NEED

- duplicated page
- card stock
- bricks (or foam bricks) at least 8 inches wide
- acrylic paint
- craft paint brushes
- pointed scissors or craft knives
- tape
- scrap cardboard

WHAT TO DO

1. Duplicate the pattern to card stock. Have the students cut out the centers of the letters with pointed scissors or craft knives.
2. Each student should place the stencil on a brick and tape it to hold it securely while painting. Show how to dab paint inside the letter stencils to form the word "conqueror."
3. Say, **The bricks remind us of the wall of Jericho. God's people didn't have to touch the wall— God caused it to**

conquerors

WHAT TO DO, CONTINUED

➤ **fall down. The wall fell down after the people did exactly what God told them to do. God is willing to knock down our walls of trouble, too.**

CHAPTER 4

God Takes Care of Us

MEMORY VERSE

Then Nebuchadnezzar said, "Praise be to the God of Shadrach, Meshach and Abednego, who has sent his angel and rescued his servants! They trusted in him."
DANIEL 3:28

✱ Turn Up the Heat ✱

King Nebuchadnezzar had a golden statue that was ninety feet tall and nine feet wide. The king commanded that all people should bow down and worship the king's idol when they heard the call-to-worship music. If someone did not bow down when the music sounded, that person would be thrown into a blazing furnace.

One day some of the king's men came to him with a disturbing report: "There are some Jews in Babylon who refuse to bow down to your statue."

The King ordered that these Jews—Shadrach, Meshach, and Abednego—be brought to him.

"Is it true that you three do not bow and worship my gods?" the king asked them. "I will give you one more chance. When you hear the music, bow down and worship my god. If you do not, I will have you thrown into the fire. No god will be able to rescue you then."

"We will not bow to your false god," the men answered. "Even if you throw us into a fire, our God is able to save us."

The king was furious. He ordered that the furnace be heated seven times hotter than usual. "Bind them and throw them into the furnace," he commanded his soldiers.

The soldiers tied up Shadrach, Meshach, and Abednego and threw them into the furnace. The furnace was so hot that the flames killed the soliders as they tossed the three men inside.

King Nebuchadnezzar sat down to watch the event. Suddenly, the king leaped to his feet. "Weren't there three men thrown into the fire?" he asked.

"Of course," his advisers answered. "There were three men bound and thrown into the fire."

"Well," the king said. "I see four men walking around in the fire, unbound and unharmed. And the fourth one looks like a son of the gods!"

Nebuchadnezzar went close to the furnace and yelled, "Shadrach, Meshach, and Abednego, servants of the Most High God, come out!"

The three men came out of the fiery furnace. All the people saw that the fire had not burned their clothing or singed a single hair on their heads, and their bodies were not harmed in any way. In fact, there was not even the smell of fire on them!

King Nebuchadnezzar had a change of heart. "Praise be to the God of Shadrach, Meshach, and Abednego, who has sent His angel and rescued His servants from the fiery furnace!" he said. "These men trusted in their God. They were willing to give up their lives rather than serve or worship any god except their own God. No one in all the land must say anything against the God of Shadrach, Meshach, and Abednego!"

BASED ON DANIEL CHAPTER 3

Discussion Questions

1. How did Shadrach, Meshach, and Abenego know it was wrong to worship the king's god?
2. We are fortunate to live in a place where we can worship God freely. But what kinds of "hot" situations have you gotten into when you've had to stand up for God's ways?

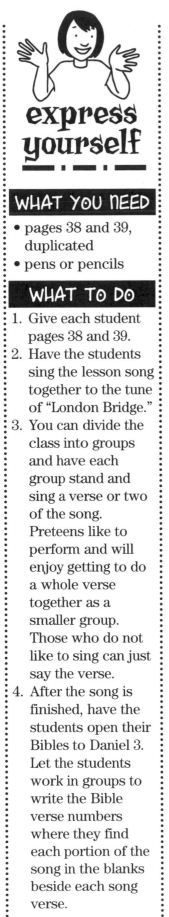

express yourself

WHAT YOU NEED

- pages 38 and 39, duplicated
- pens or pencils

WHAT TO DO

1. Give each student pages 38 and 39.
2. Have the students sing the lesson song together to the tune of "London Bridge."
3. You can divide the class into groups and have each group stand and sing a verse or two of the song. Preteens like to perform and will enjoy getting to do a whole verse together as a smaller group. Those who do not like to sing can just say the verse.
4. After the song is finished, have the students open their Bibles to Daniel 3. Let the students work in groups to write the Bible verse numbers where they find each portion of the song in the blanks beside each song verse.

takes care

∗ Sing Out! ∗

Nebuchadnezzar made an image of gold,
Image of gold,
Image of gold.
Nebuchadnezzar made an image of gold
And said that all must worship.

_____

When music sounded, all must bow,
All must bow,
All must bow.
When music sounded, all must bow.
The king said all must worship me.

_____

Three men refused to bow to an idol,
Bow to an idol,
Bow to an idol,
Three men refused to bow to an idol.
They would only worship God.

_____

The three said, "Our God will keep us safe,
Keep us safe,
Keep us safe."
The three said, "Our God will keep us safe.
But even if not, we'll not worship you."

_____

Heat the oven seven times hotter,
Seven times hotter,
Seven times hotter.
Heat the oven seven times hotter,
The king ordered his men.

_____

The king had them bound and thrown into the fire,
Thrown into the fire,
Thrown into the fire.
The king had them bound and thrown into the fire,
Because they wouldn't worship him.

———————————————

The King saw four men walking in the fire,
Walking in the fire,
Walking in the fire.
The King saw four men walking in the fire.
Who was the fourth man?

———————————————

It must be the Son of God,
The Son of God,
The Son of God.
It must be the Son of God.
Nebuchadnezzar told the
men to come out.

———————————————

Shadrach, Meshach,
Abednego came out of the
furnace,
Came out of the furnace,
Came out of the furnace.
Shadrach, Meshach, Abednego came out of the furnace.
They didn't even smell like smoke.

———————————————

The king said, "Praise be to the only God,
The only God,
The only God."
The king said, "Praise be to the only God.
From now on we'll worship the only God!"

———————————————

* A King Learns *
a Lesson

Officials in Babylon
(Daniel 3:1-3)
satraps
prefects
governors
advisers
treasurers
judges
magistrates

Call to Worship
(Daniel 3:7)
Horn
Flute
Zither
Lyre
Harp
Pipes

Young men who wouldn't worship the idol
(Daniel 3:12)
Shadrach
Meshach
Abednego

Items the fire did not harm
(Daniel 3:27)
Bodies
Hair
Robes

King who learned a lesson
(Daniel 3:1, 28)
Nebuchadnezzar

```
J  R  Z  I  T  H  E  R  B  E  D  S  T  O
G  O  V  E  R  N  O  R  S  N  T  E  Q  R
V  N  H  G  P  F  G  R  S  N  I  T  R  O
R  S  A  T  R  A  P  S  N  Z  Z  A  L  K
I  O  R  O  B  E  S  S  E  T  P  R  U  N
A  N  P  I  P  E  S  X  B  M  B  T  L  I
H  O  R  N  E  S  E  T  U  L  F  S  M  N
Q  J  U  D  G  E  S  A  C  A  M  I  F  R
J  U  D  B  N  M  O  H  H  H  V  G  O  M
T  S  R  E  S  I  V  D  A  U  Y  A  H  E
P  L  U  A  M  B  X  I  D  D  O  M  C  S
B  B  E  B  E  D  R  O  N  U  P  Q  A  H
O  T  R  E  A  S  U  R  E  R  S  A  R  A
D  O  O  D  O  O  R  A  Z  A  B  B  D  C
I  U  O  N  E  B  A  A  Z  A  R  Q  A  H
E  E  E  E  R  U  N  S  A  B  R  O  H  H
S  G  O  G  N  O  L  Y  R  E  N  O  S  E
J  E  S  O  P  R  E  F  E  C  T  S  R  G
```

✳ Trust Beaded Mobile ✳

craft

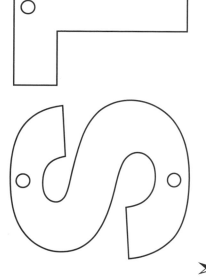

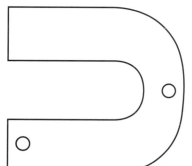

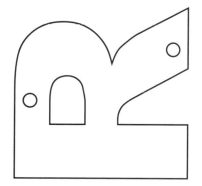

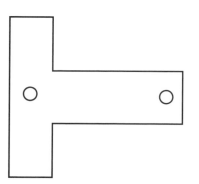

WHAT YOU NEED

- duplicated page
- colorful card stock
- plastic lacing
- scissors
- pony beads
- tape
- markers
- hole punch

WHAT TO DO, CONTINUED

➤ 6. Then have each student tie one end of a length of lacing through the bottom hole in the T, then thread four or five beads onto the lacing and tie the end through the top hole in the R.

7. Each student should repeat Step 7 until all the letters have been connected to form the word "trust." Each student also can add a length of lacing to the bottom of the last "T," thread some beads on to the lacing and tie the lacing around the last bead to hold on all the beads.

8. Say, **We have many times in our lives when we need to trust God. Use the markers to write at least one word on each of your mobile letters that describes a time when you trusted God.** Suggest: afraid, sick, hurt by a friend, tempted, etc.

9. Say, **Hang up your mobiles at home to remember that we can trust our Awesome God in every situation in our lives.**

WHAT TO DO

1. Give each student a pattern page. You will need 20 or more beads per student.
2. Have the students cut the letters from the page.
3. Have each student punch a hole in each letter where indicated.
4. Instruct the students to cut the plastic lacing in 6-inch lengths or longer. Each student will need five lengths of lacing.
5. Construct the mobile by tying a length of lacing through the top hole of one of the T's, then tie it into a loop to form a hanger.

takes care

✳ Fire Diorama ✳

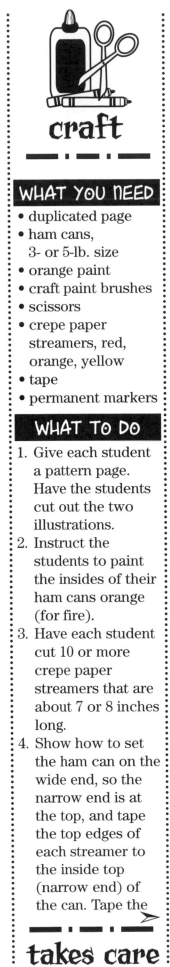

WHAT YOU NEED

- duplicated page
- ham cans,
  3- or 5-lb. size
- orange paint
- craft paint brushes
- scissors
- crepe paper
  streamers, red,
  orange, yellow
- tape
- permanent markers

WHAT TO DO

1. Give each student
   a pattern page.
   Have the students
   cut out the two
   illustrations.
2. Instruct the
   students to paint
   the insides of their
   ham cans orange
   (for fire).
3. Have each student
   cut 10 or more
   crepe paper
   streamers that are
   about 7 or 8 inches
   long.
4. Show how to set
   the ham can on the
   wide end, so the
   narrow end is at
   the top, and tape
   the top edges of
   each streamer to
   the inside top
   (narrow end) of
   the can. Tape the

takes care

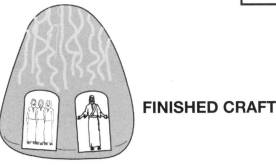

FINISHED CRAFT

WHAT TO DO, CONTINUED

➤ streamers in layers from back to front, so they hang down and cover most of the inside of the can to look like flames.

5. Have the students fold the tabs on each of their figures to the back. They should tape the tabs to the bottoms of the cans (floor of diorama) by placing the tape at the back and front of each figure to hold them securely.
6. The students can use permanent markers to write the memory verse on the outsides of their dioramas.

* God Vs. Idols *

Spent 20 minutes reading my Bible.	Gave part of my chore money for an offering at church.	Used all of my allowance to buy a new CD.
Begged my parents to let me go to a ball game instead of church.	Bought concert tickets with the money I was saving to give to a mission project.	Used our youth group money to buy pizza, instead of Bibles to send to inner-city missions as planned.
Couldn't tell the guy or girl I like that I go to church for fear he or she would think I'm not cool.	Used bad language in front of my friends to look tough.	Bad-mouthed my parents because my friends do it to theirs.
Lied and told my mom I was going to the library, but instead went to a movie she didn't want me to see.	Left a new kid at school out of our lunch group because my friends might not like him or her.	Was disrespectful to a teacher to impress others in my class.

game

WHAT YOU NEED
- duplicated page
- scissors
- index cards
- bag or sack

WHAT TO DO
1. Cut the phrases from the page. Glue one phrase to each of twelve index cards. (If your class is large, make two sets of cards.)
2. Put the cards inside a bag.
3. Have the students take turns pulling a card out of the bag, and reading the phrases out loud.
4. Say, **When you think the person reading the card is worshipping God, stand up, raise your hands to God, and shout, "Praise to God!" When you think the person reading the card is worshipping idols, stand up, fold your arms across your chest like a statue, and shake your head.**

takes care

43

bulletin board

WHAT YOU NEED
- duplicated page
- green paper
- scissors
- stapler
- magazines
- plain paper
- markers

WHAT TO DO

1. Duplicate the pattern to green paper. Make several copies.
2. Make a bulletin board heading by writing "Creeping Idols" on paper.
3. Use scissors to cut vine-like strips. Have the students cut out the leaves from the pattern pages.
4. Fasten the vines and leaves to the bulletin board with a stapler.
5. Have the students cut from magazines pictures of things they might worship instead of God. Suggest: movies, clothes, music, electronics, celebrities, etc.
6. Have each student fasten a picture below each leaf on the bulletin board ➤

takes care

* Creeping Idols *

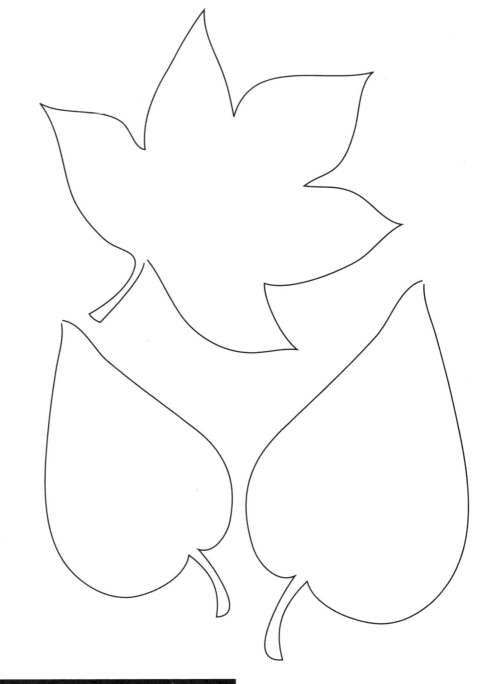

WHAT TO DO, CONTINUED

➤ and write the name of each potential idol on a leaf.

7. Say, **We don't usually start out to worship idols or put other things or people before God. But sometimes we think "just this once." Then it becomes easier and easier to put other things before God. Soon, the "idols" take over our lives like a vine that grows and creeps up a wall or over a fence. Let's pray and ask God to help us keep the creeping idols out of our lives so we can better live for Him.**

* The Un-treasure * Hunt

THE UNITED STATES OF AMERICA

I 68458156 f

ONE

I 68458156 f

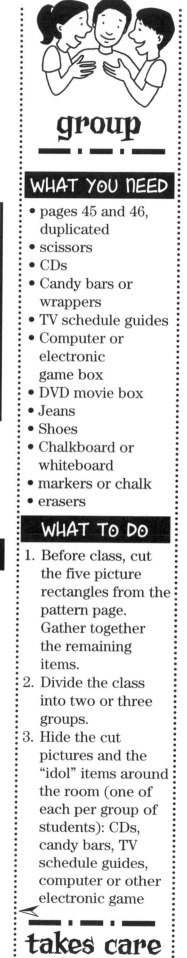

group

WHAT YOU NEED

- pages 45 and 46, duplicated
- scissors
- CDs
- Candy bars or wrappers
- TV schedule guides
- Computer or electronic game box
- DVD movie box
- Jeans
- Shoes
- Chalkboard or whiteboard
- markers or chalk
- erasers

WHAT TO DO

1. Before class, cut the five picture rectangles from the pattern page. Gather together the remaining items.
2. Divide the class into two or three groups.
3. Hide the cut pictures and the "idol" items around the room (one of each per group of students): CDs, candy bars, TV schedule guides, computer or other electronic game

takes care

WHAT TO DO, CONTINUED

➤ boxes, DVD movie boxes, jeans and shoes.
4. Write the items on a chalkboard or whiteboard, one list for each team.

money	jewelry	electronic games
Rock Star magazine	CDs	new movies
motorcycle	candy	great clothes
sports car	TV	the latest shoes

5. Say, **Each group should look around the room for the items listed on the board. As you find each item, erase the word from the board. If you find a second copy of the same item, put that item back for the other team(s) to find, When you have found all the items, place them on your table and wait for everyone to finish.**
6. Spend some time discussing how each of the items can become an idol when put before God. Say, **Things we treasure are not bad to want or enjoy. But we must be careful not to put them before God. When we begin to worship things instead of God, our treasures become "un-treasures," or idols.**

CHAPTER 5

God Guides Us by His Word

 MEMORY VERSE

Carefully follow all the words of this law, which are written in this book.

DEUTERONOMY 28:58

✳ Read the Instructions ✳

God wants us to know His Word. He took great care in choosing the writers for each book in the Bible. God inspired every word that was written on every page.

Our memory verse is from Deuteronomy, where Moses retells how God led His people out of slavery and through the wilderness to the Promised Land. Then Moses explains the Ten Commandments and other laws for godly living. One of the most important rules, says Moses, is that we use the Bible as our guide.

The Bible contains other examples of God's desire that we use His Word in our daily lives. For example, 2 Timothy 3:16 tells us that all Scripture is God-breathed and should be used to teach others. Also, the beginning of Revelation reads, "Blessed is the one who reads the Words of God and takes them to heart." So not only does God want us to teach from the Bible, He wants us to have the Bible in our hearts and minds so that it affects everything we do.

To help the Bible seep deeply into your life, investigate the following questions:

• What are the first few words of the Bible? What is the last word in the Bible?

• Find the Ten Commandments in Deuteronomy. Where in Exodus do they also appear?

• Look for the book of Psalms. This is the longest book in the Bible. How many chapters does it have?

• Find a "praise chapter" you like in Psalms and tell what you like about it.

• Find the story of Jesus' birth, and then of His death and resurrection.

• Find a lesson in Paul's letters or from another letter writer in the New Testament.

God thought of everything when he gave us the Bible. He wants us to learn, remember and use his wonderful Word to help us in our everyday lives.

BASED ON DEUTERONOMY 26:16-19; 28; LUKE 1:1-4; 2 TIMOTHY 3:16; REVELATION 1:1-3

❓ Discussion Questions

1. Why do you think God gave us the Bible?

2. If we did not have the Bible, in what other ways would you know that God and Jesus exist?

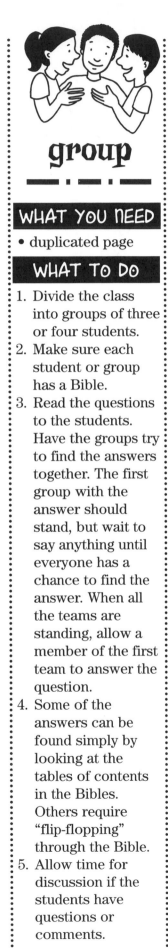

group

WHAT YOU NEED

• duplicated page

WHAT TO DO

1. Divide the class into groups of three or four students.
2. Make sure each student or group has a Bible.
3. Read the questions to the students. Have the groups try to find the answers together. The first group with the answer should stand, but wait to say anything until everyone has a chance to find the answer. When all the teams are standing, allow a member of the first team to answer the question.
4. Some of the answers can be found simply by looking at the tables of contents in the Bibles. Others require "flip-flopping" through the Bible.
5. Allow time for discussion if the students have questions or comments.

His Word

* Flip Flop * Bible Search

How many books are in the Bible?

How many sections are in the Bible?

What is the name of the first book in the New Testament?

What are the first three words in the Bible?

What is the last word in the Bible?

What does 2 Timothy 3:16 say about the Scriptures?

Name the books of the Gospels of Christ.

How many chapters are in the book of Psalms?

What is the last book in the Old Testament?

Finish this book title: "Song of _____"

Which of the four gospels begins with the same three words that begin Genesis?

How many books in the New Testament are called "John"?

Which book comes after Psalms?

What is the name of the last book in the Bible?

Which book gives the number of people in each of the 12 tribes of Israel?

Which prophet does Mark quote in chapter 1, verse 2?

Which two men's births are predicted in Luke 1?

In John 20:31, why are "these things written?"

Revelation 1:3 says we are blessed when we do what?

According to Psalm 118, verses 1-4, what endures forever?

Matthew 1 tells the genealogy of whom?

What is the last sentence in the book of Nehemiah?

* A Trip through * the Bible

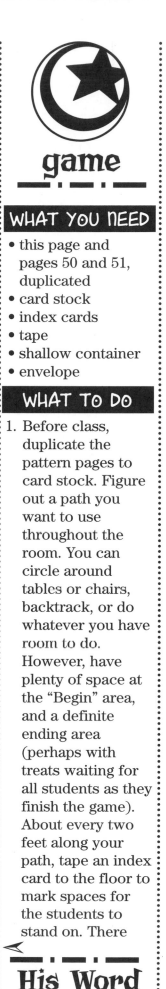

WHAT YOU NEED

- this page and pages 50 and 51, duplicated
- card stock
- index cards
- tape
- shallow container
- envelope

Which day did God create people? Find the answer in Genesis 1:31, and move that number of spaces ahead.	How many days did it rain during the great Flood? Find the answer in Genesis 7:17, divide that number by 4, then subtract 6; move ahead the number of remaining spaces.
God made a covenant with Abram, as Genesis 15 tells us. Look in Genesis 15:9 to see the ages of the goat, ram, and heifer that Abram was to prepare for a sacrifice. Move that many spaces forward.	Find the names of Jacob's twin sons in Genesis 25:34-36. Add the number of letters in their names and divide that number by three. Move ahead that many spaces.
How many of Jacob's 12 sons had a mother named Rachel? Find the answer in Genesis 35:24 and move ahead that many spaces.	In Exodus 2:2, we are told how many months Moses' mother hid him before placing him in a basket in the Nile. Move ahead that many spaces.

WHAT TO DO

1. Before class, duplicate the pattern pages to card stock. Figure out a path you want to use throughout the room. You can circle around tables or chairs, backtrack, or do whatever you have room to do. However, have plenty of space at the "Begin" area, and a definite ending area (perhaps with treats waiting for all students as they finish the game). About every two feet along your path, tape an index card to the floor to mark spaces for the students to stand on. There

WHAT TO DO, CONTINUED

➤ should be 50 spaces. Finally, cut the 30 cards from the pattern pages that you duplicated to card stock.

2. To play the game, mix up the cards, and place them face down inside a shallow container. Have all the students gather at the "Begin" area. Have each student carry a Bible.

3. Have one student begin the game by taking a card. The student should read the phrase, then look in the Bible for instructions on how to proceed and read them aloud. After the first student has figured out how to proceed, a second student should draw a card and read the phrase, look in the Bible for instructions, and complete his or her turn. Repeat until at least one student has finished the entire game path. You can play until all of the students have completed the path, if time allows. (Gather the used cards and hold them in case you run out of cards in the container before the game is finished, then shuffle them and start over.)

His Word

Joshua sent this many spies into the land God promised them. Joshua 2:1 tells the answer. Move ahead that many spaces.	Joshua 6:13 says this many priests carried this many trumpets. Move this number of spaces forward, just as God commanded His people to do when they marched around the city of Jericho.	In Jeremiah 7:24, God is angry because His people have gone which direction? Move 3 spaces in that direction.
Which day did God create plants and trees? Find the answer in Genesis 1:11-13, and move that number of spaces ahead.	1 Samuel 7:1-2 tells how many years the ark of the covenant, precious to God and His people, remained under the care of Abinadab's son because the Israelites were sinful. Divide that number by 5, and move ahead that number of spaces.	David took this many stones to fight against Goliath. Find the answer in 1 Samuel 17:40. Subtract 4, and move backward that many spaces.
How many times did God tell Naaman to dip in the Jordan River to be healed from leprosy? 2 Kings 5:14 gives the answer. Move ahead that number of spaces.	In 2 Kings 12, King Joash had the God's temple repaired. How old was Joash when he became king? Look in 2 Kings 11:21 for the answer. Move ahead that many spaces.	How many friends came to comfort Job when he had troubles? Move one space for each friend. Job 2:11 gives the answer.
How many times each day does the writer of Psalm 119:164 praise God? Move ahead that many spaces.	Move 3 spaces in the direction that Proverbs 4:25 says to keep our eyes.	For how many years were Daniel, Shadrach, Meshach, and Abednego to be trained in Babylon, as mentioned in Daniel 1:5? Move ahead that number of spaces.

How many men did King Nebuchadnezzar see walking around in the furnace after he had thrown in Shadrach, Meshach, and Abednego? Daniel 3:25 tells the number of spaces you should move forward.	Find the number in Jonah 1:17 that tells how many days Jonah spent in the great fish's belly. Move ahead that number of spaces.	How many days and nights did Jesus fast before He was tempted in the desert? Divide the number found in Matthew 4:2 by 10 and move ahead that number of spaces.
How old was Jesus when Mary and Joseph thought He was lost, when He really was in God's temple asking questions of the teachers? Find the answer in Luke 2:42. Divide by two and move ahead twice that many spaces.	Matthew 14:17 tells how much food the disciples found to feed a large crowd of people. Add together the two numbers given and move that many spaces ahead.	In Matthew 25:14-15, add up the number of talents the man gave to his servants. Move ahead that many spaces.
Which direction did some disciples turn in John 6:66? Move 2 spaces in this direction.	Mark 12:42 says that a widow put her very last coins—this many—in the temple treasury. Move that number of spaces ahead. Be generous and invite the person closest behind you up to where you land.	Read the verse in Mark 14:30. How many times did Jesus say Peter would disown him? Move that many spaces forward.
How many healed men did not come back to thank Jesus in Luke 17:17? Move back that number of spaces, then move forward the number of men that Jesus cleansed.	Jesus' first miracle was turning water into wine at a wedding, in John 2. John 2:6 reveals how many stone jars Jesus said to fill with water. Move ahead that many spaces. Since a wedding is a happy occasion, tell the two people farthest behind to catch up to you.	Acts 6:3 gives the number of godly men chosen to take responsibility in the early church. Find the number of men chosen, then move ahead that many spaces.

craft

WHAT YOU NEED
- duplicated page
- card stock
- pens or markers
- scissors
- clear, self-stick plastic
- Bible concordances

WHAT TO DO
1. Give each student a pattern page.
2. Have the students cut the card from the page.
3. Say, **Many times we get a new electronic gadget that has a "quick-reference" card to get us started in using the item, or to help when we're having difficulty operating the gadget. We can all use a quick-card when it comes to finding verses in the Bible to answer our questions or help us in a situation.**
4. Have the students use their Bibles and a concordance to write more quick-references on the backs of their Quick Reference Cards.

His Word

Quick Reference Card

Anger
Matthew 5:21-26

Worry
Matthew 6:25-34

Fear
Luke 12:4-7

Forgiving
Matthew 18:21-22

Am I Forgiven?
1 John 2:12

Am I Loved?
John 3:16

Judging Others
Luke 6:37-42

Love my enemies?
Matthew 5:43-48

When I am tempted
1 Corinthians 10:13

✳ Journaling ✳ Through the Bible

NO

U

TURNS from the Word

O B E Y

DO NOT ENTER INTO SIN

STOP AND PRAY FOR GUIDANCE

HEAVEN

ONE WAY TO

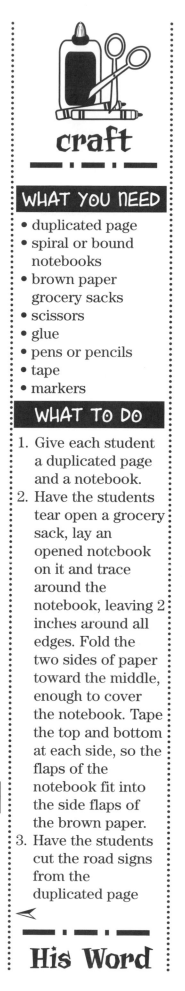

craft

WHAT YOU NEED

- duplicated page
- spiral or bound notebooks
- brown paper grocery sacks
- scissors
- glue
- pens or pencils
- tape
- markers

WHAT TO DO

1. Give each student a duplicated page and a notebook.
2. Have the students tear open a grocery sack, lay an opened notcbook on it and trace around the notebook, leaving 2 inches around all edges. Fold the two sides of paper toward the middle, enough to cover the notebook. Tape the top and bottom at each side, so the flaps of the notebook fit into the side flaps of the brown paper.
3. Have the students cut the road signs from the duplicated page

His Word

WHAT TO DO, CONTINUED

➤ and glue them onto the fronts of their covered journals.

4. Say, **God wants us to know His Word. He gives us guidance for every situation in the Bible, just like road signs guide us along the way. You can use your journals as you read God's Word. Keep track of the chapters and stories you read in the Bible. Make notes, write favorite verses, write a poem or prayer to God, or write whatever you want in your journal.**

puzzle

WHAT YOU NEED

- duplicated page
- pens or pencils
- highlighter pens

WHAT TO DO

1. Give each student a duplicated page. Have plenty of Bibles available.
2. Tell the students to follow the path and discover the names of all 66 books of the Bible. Each student should put a pencil line after each name of a book in the Bible.
3. After the students finish finding all the books of the Bible, have them highlight the memory verse that follows the listing of books.
4. Say, **God carefully planned His Word so we would have it always for guidance.** "Carefully follow," God tells us.

His Word

CHAPTER 6

God Encourages Us to Live Godly Lives

MEMORY VERSE

"I will put my law in their minds and write it on their hearts. I will be their God, and they will be my people."

JEREMIAH 31:33

✱ God's Messengers ✱

God's people were straying from His laws and His Word. God needed a way to tell His people that they were heading down the wrong path. He wanted to warn the people that their sinful ways were going to bring destruction upon them.

God chose certain people to deliver his messages. These deliverers of God's Word are called "prophets." The Old Testament has 17 books of prophecy. The prophet Jeremiah wrote the books of Jeremiah and Lamentations.

In Jeremiah 30:2, God says to Jeremiah, "Write in a book all the words I have spoken to you." God wanted His people to have these words to read and remember, so that they would know they needed to stop sinning and follow His ways.

As we look through Jeremiah 30, many times we see the phrases, "This is what the Lord says" and "declares the Lord." God spoke to Jeremiah and expected Jeremiah to deliver His Word to the people of Israel. In His messages, God reminded His people of His love, His care for them, and His expectations that they obey His laws.

God promises to lead his people, deliver them from their sins, and forgive them. God says He longs to have a good relationship with His people, which include us today. In order to have a good relationship with God, His people need to get rid of their sin and do their best to follow His laws.

Through his prophets, God promised a covenant with His people. He declared that He would put His law in their minds and write it on their hearts. It is very important to God that we remember to follow His laws.

"I will be their God and they will be My people," God said about the Israelites and of all His chosen people—including us!

BASED ON JEREMIAH 30 AND 31

Discussion Questions

1. Why did God need to deliver His Word to His chosen people?
2. How does God deliver His Word today?

* Class Reading *

WHAT YOU NEED
- duplicated page
- Bibles

WHAT TO DO

1. Divide the class into small groups. Give each group a duplicated page.
2. Have each group look up and write down one of the listed verses.
3. Go around and have one member of each group read that group's verse.
4. Say, **God used the prophets to deliver His Word to the people who were straying from Him and His will. God wants us to obey Him. He longs to be our God and have us be His people.**
5. Discuss ways we can show God that we want to be His people.

Godly Lives

Isaiah 1:1

Ezekiel 1:1-3

Daniel 1:1-4, 17

Hosea 1:1

Joel 1:1

Amos 1:1

Obadiah 1:1

Jonah 1:1-2

Micah 1:1-2

Nahum 1:1

Habakkuk 1:1

Zephaniah 1:1

Haggai 1:1

Zechariah 1:1

Malachi 1:1

* Bubble Wrap * Heart Cards

I will put my law in their minds and write it on their hearts. I will be their God, and they will be my people.

Jeremiah 31:33

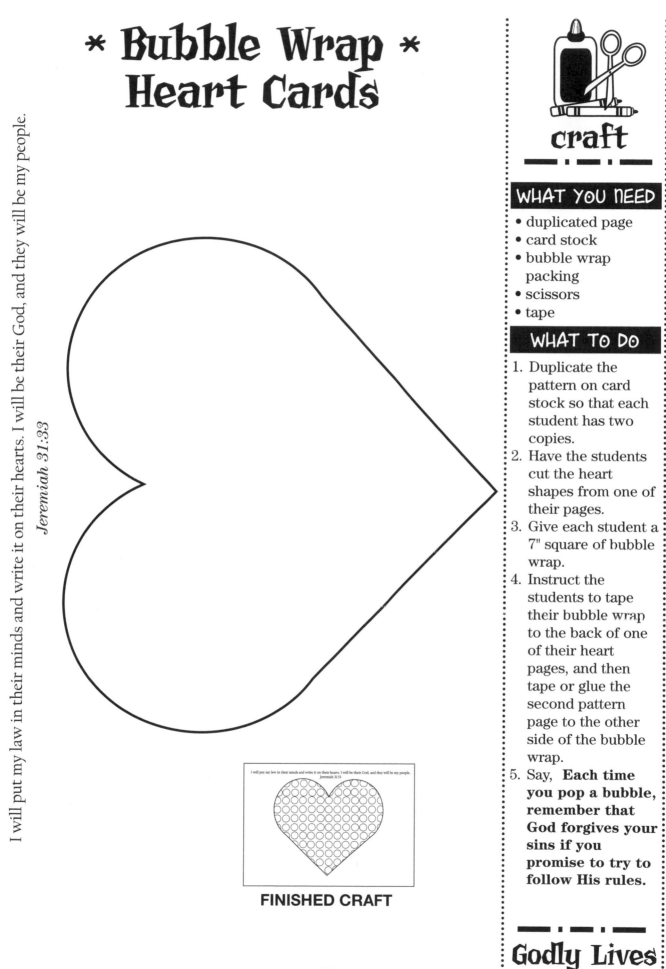

FINISHED CRAFT

craft

WHAT YOU NEED

- duplicated page
- card stock
- bubble wrap packing
- scissors
- tape

WHAT TO DO

1. Duplicate the pattern on card stock so that each student has two copies.
2. Have the students cut the heart shapes from one of their pages.
3. Give each student a 7" square of bubble wrap.
4. Instruct the students to tape their bubble wrap to the back of one of their heart pages, and then tape or glue the second pattern page to the other side of the bubble wrap.
5. Say, **Each time you pop a bubble, remember that God forgives your sins if you promise to try to follow His rules.**

Godly Lives

✻ God Gives a Promise ✻

WHAT YOU NEED

- duplicated page
- pens or pencils
- Bibles

WHAT TO DO

1. Give each student a puzzle page.
2. Say, **When we allow God to put His law in our minds and write it on our hearts, He gives us a promise. Use the heart symbols to find the correct letter to put in each blank below.**

HEART KEY

1 heart = A
2 hearts = E
3 hearts = I
4 hearts = O

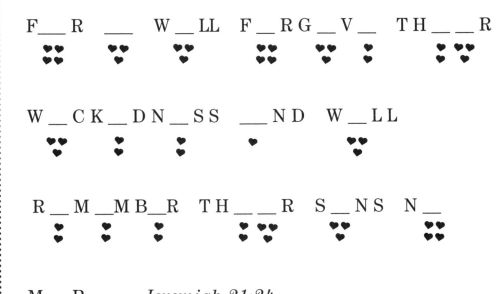

F__R __ W__LL F__RG__V__ TH____R

W__CK__DN__SS __ND W__LL

R__M__MB__R TH____R S__NS N__

M__ R__. —*Jeremiah 31:34*

Special Delivery

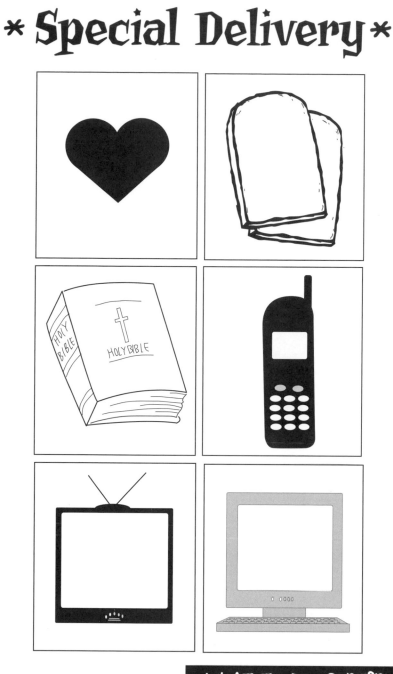

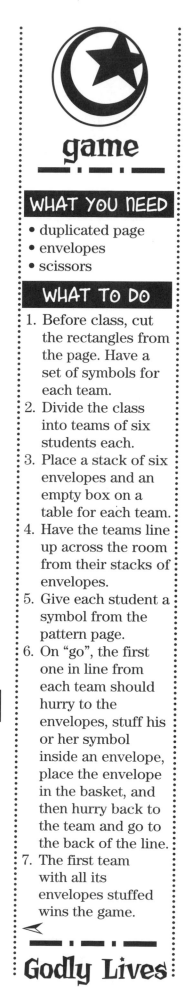

game

WHAT YOU NEED

- duplicated page
- envelopes
- scissors

WHAT TO DO

1. Before class, cut the rectangles from the page. Have a set of symbols for each team.
2. Divide the class into teams of six students each.
3. Place a stack of six envelopes and an empty box on a table for each team.
4. Have the teams line up across the room from their stacks of envelopes.
5. Give each student a symbol from the pattern page.
6. On "go", the first one in line from each team should hurry to the envelopes, stuff his or her symbol inside an envelope, place the envelope in the basket, and then hurry back to the team and go to the back of the line.
7. The first team with all its envelopes stuffed wins the game.

WHAT TO DO, CONTINUED

➤ 8. After the game is over, have the teams pull the symbols from the envelopes. Ask for volunteers to tell how each symbol relates to the Bible lesson (see below).

Heart: God puts His law in our hearts and minds
Ten Commandments: God's Law
Bible: We use the Bible to find out what God expects from us
Telephone: We can use our telephones to spread God's Word
Television: Another way of communicating God's Word to people
Computer: More modern way of communicating God's Word

Godly Lives

express yourself

WHAT YOU NEED

- duplicated page
- pens or pencils

WHAT TO DO

1. Give each student a "Dear God" page.
2. Say, **Our awesome God loves us very much. He wants to be our God and wants us to be His people. God sent the prophets to encourage His people to live godly lives.**
3. Say, **Finish the paragraphs on the diary page. Then write a poem or prayer to God at the bottom of the page.**

Godly Lives

✱ Dear God Diary Page ✱

Dear God, I am so thankful that You want me to be one of Your people. I am going to try to live a more godly life by _____

God, I know You want me to have Your law in my mind and my heart. I promise to read Your Word ___ minutes each day.

Other areas of my life that I can keep godly for you are:

- Music. I promise to _____
- Movies/television shows. I promise to

_____

- Attitudes toward others. I promise to

_____

- Things others may try to get me to do that I know are wrong, such as _____

My own thoughts

_____

_____

_____

* God's Message *

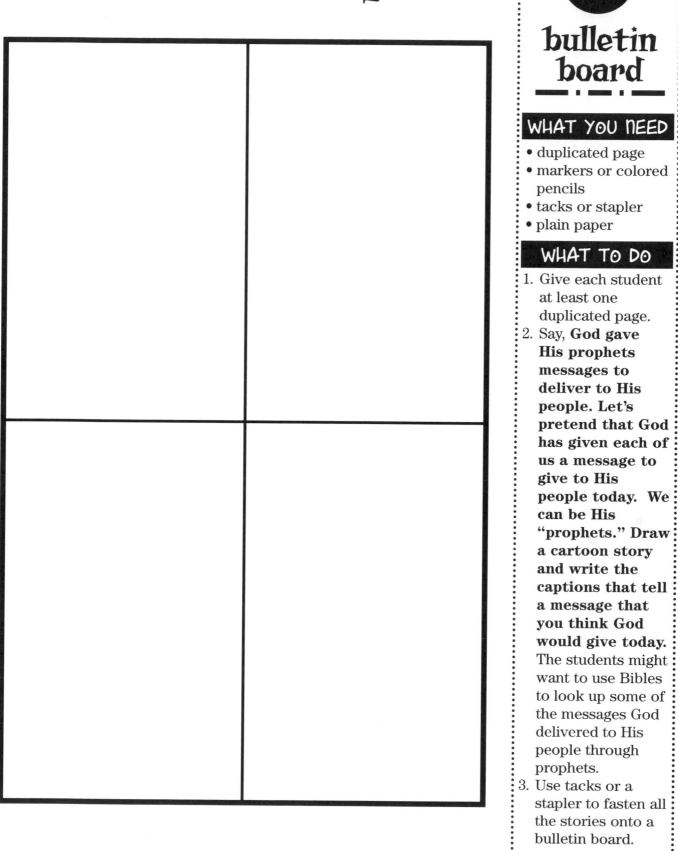

WHAT YOU NEED

- duplicated page
- markers or colored pencils
- tacks or stapler
- plain paper

WHAT TO DO

1. Give each student at least one duplicated page.
2. Say, **God gave His prophets messages to deliver to His people. Let's pretend that God has given each of us a message to give to His people today. We can be His "prophets." Draw a cartoon story and write the captions that tell a message that you think God would give today.** The students might want to use Bibles to look up some of the messages God delivered to His people through prophets.
3. Use tacks or a stapler to fasten all the stories onto a bulletin board.

Godly Lives

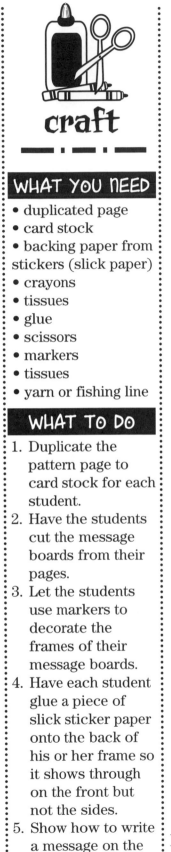

craft

WHAT YOU NEED

- duplicated page
- card stock
- backing paper from stickers (slick paper)
- crayons
- tissues
- glue
- scissors
- markers
- tissues
- yarn or fishing line

WHAT TO DO

1. Duplicate the pattern page to card stock for each student.
2. Have the students cut the message boards from their pages.
3. Let the students use markers to decorate the frames of their message boards.
4. Have each student glue a piece of slick sticker paper onto the back of his or her frame so it shows through on the front but not the sides.
5. Show how to write a message on the slick paper and easily wipe it off with a tissue.

Godly Lives

✳ Mini Erasable ✳ Memo Boards

WHAT TO DO, CONTINUED

6. Have the students attach loops of yarn or fishing line to their message boards so they can hang them in their rooms at home.
7. Say, **You can hang your message boards in your rooms at home. The message board will remind you that God sent messages to His people to remind them to live godly lives for Him.**

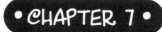

CHAPTER 7

Our Awesome God is Worthy of Our Praise

MEMORY VERSE

I call to the Lord, who is worthy of praise.
PSALM 18:3

* Praise Him *

The book of Psalms is a collection of praises mostly written by David. Each psalm expresses the author's love for God and thanks for His care and blessings.

Just because the writers praised God did not mean their lives were always happy and easy. For example, even though David was a king, he had many problems throughout his life. But he knew to turn to God for help. God was there to forgive and see David through the bad times. David continued to praise God, no matter what was happening in his life. He is a great example for us—God deserves our praise even if we are going through difficulties! He is worthy of our praise all the time.

Do you ever wonder why we should praise God? After all, isn't God perfect? So why would He need to hear our praise? Think about a time someone told you he or she loved you. Maybe it was your mom or your grandpa or a friend. You probably knew already that this person loved you. But it made you feel good to hear it, didn't it? God is the same way. He wants to hear you praise Him.

There is another reason to praise God: praising God makes you a happier, more satisfied person. When you praise God, you have to think about your life and how God is working in it. By praising Him you are saying that you know God brings you all the good in your life and helps you through all the bad. So praising God is a good reminder that you are God's child, and He is your heavenly Father.

Why don't you take a minute right now to praise God? Say, shout, or sing, "I love You, Lord!"

BASED ON PSALM 18:1-3, 1 CHRONICLES 16:25; 2 SAMUEL 22:4

Discussion Questions

?

1. Why do you think the book of Psalms is in the Bible?
2. How do you praise God?

* It Bears Repeating *

COLUMN A	COLUMN B
Psalm 18:1-3	2 Samuel 22:50
Psalm 96:4-6	Psalm 145:3
Psalm 48:1	Psalm 146:1
1 Kings 8:15	2 Chronicles 6:4
Psalm 18:49	2 Samuel 22:2-4
Psalm 103:1	1 Chronicles 16:25

✳ Sing Praises ✳

I call to the Lord,
I call to the Lord,
I call to the Lord,
Who is worthy of praise. (Psalm 18:3)

Lord, You are very great,
Lord, You are very great,
Lord, You are very great,
O Lord my God. (Psalm 104:1)

Shout for joy to the Lord,
Shout for joy to the Lord,
Shout for joy to the Lord,
All the earth. (Psalm 100:1)

Praise His holy name,
Praise His holy name,
Praise His holy name,
Sing and praise His holy name. (Psalm 30:4)

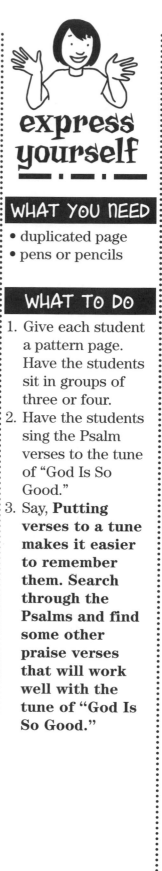

express yourself

WHAT YOU NEED

- duplicated page
- pens or pencils

WHAT TO DO

1. Give each student a pattern page. Have the students sit in groups of three or four.
2. Have the students sing the Psalm verses to the tune of "God Is So Good."
3. Say, **Putting verses to a tune makes it easier to remember them. Search through the Psalms and find some other praise verses that will work well with the tune of "God Is So Good."**

praise

Ribbon Key Holder

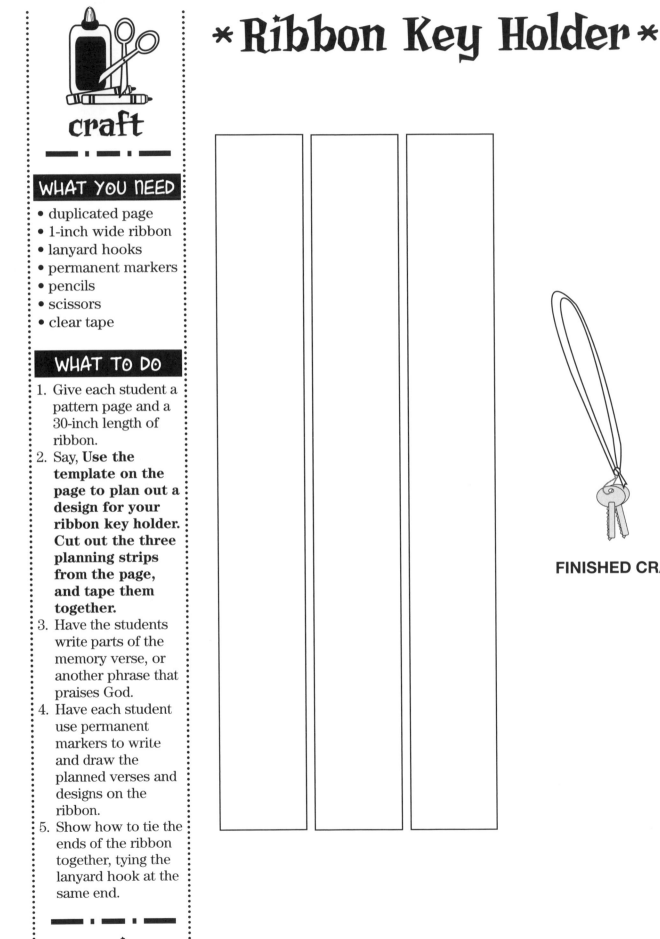

WHAT YOU NEED

- duplicated page
- 1-inch wide ribbon
- lanyard hooks
- permanent markers
- pencils
- scissors
- clear tape

WHAT TO DO

1. Give each student a pattern page and a 30-inch length of ribbon.
2. Say, **Use the template on the page to plan out a design for your ribbon key holder. Cut out the three planning strips from the page, and tape them together.**
3. Have the students write parts of the memory verse, or another phrase that praises God.
4. Have each student use permanent markers to write and draw the planned verses and designs on the ribbon.
5. Show how to tie the ends of the ribbon together, tying the lanyard hook at the same end.

FINISHED CRAFT

praise

✴ Praise Quilt ✴

craft

WHAT YOU NEED

- pages 67 and 68 duplicated
- card stock
- white cotton handkerchiefs, at least 12 x 12 inches
- crayons
- iron
- towel
- plain paper
- yarn
- large plastic needles
- scissors

WHAT TO DO

1. Duplicate the pattern pages on card stock, making several copies per student. Cut many 6-inch lengths of yarn for "sewing."
2. Heat the iron to medium, and place a folded towel on the counter next to the iron. Warn the students to stay away from the hot iron.
3. Give each student a handkerchief and a sheet of paper.
4. Let the students design their own "praise" quilt squares on the paper, which will

praise

WHAT TO DO, CONTINUED

➤ become iron-on transfers. Students can freehand their designs, or they can cut out shapes from the pattern, color them, and glue them to the paper. Either way, all designs should be colored with crayons to make the transfer.

5. If the students want to write on their quilt squares, they should write the words backwards so they will transfer properly to the quilt.
6. Iron the transfers onto the handkerchiefs for the students.
7. Lay all the handkerchiefs on a table to form a quilt. Overlap the hemmed edges of the handkerchiefs because this is where the squares will be attached together.
8. Have each student thread a 6-inch length of yarn though a plastic needle.
9. Show how to use a needle to make one stitch through a corner of the overlapped quilt squares so that both ends of the yarn are on the topside. When the whole quilt is sewed together, remove the needle from the yarn and tie the yarn ends together in a knot.
10. Display your finished quilt in your classroom, or in an area of the building where all can enjoy it.

68

FINISHED CRAFT

My Own Psalm

express yourself

WHAT YOU NEED

- duplicated page
- pens or pencils
- Bibles

WHAT TO DO

1. Give each student a pattern page.
2. Say, **David and other psalm writers expressed their love and praise for God. Write something to praise God, whether it be a poem, song, prayer, or a letter to God. Maybe you'd rather just write some short phrases around the page. Make it your own praise to God.**
3. The students may add their praises to their journals from Chapter 5.

praise

WHAT YOU NEED

- pages 70, 71, and 72, duplicated
- stapler
- scissors
- recipe ingredients (see below)
- plain paper
- construction paper
- glue

WHAT TO DO

1. Give each student the duplicated pages, and a few sheets of plain paper and construction paper.
2. Have the students cut out all the recipe pages and glue each page to a half-sheet of construction paper.
3. Try one of the recipes in class as a snack. Let the students enjoy making and eating the snack together. Remind them that we can praise God anytime, for anything.

✶ Praise Recipes ✶

RECIPE FOR PRAISE:

- Daily Dose of Prayer
- Continuous Respect
- Heart Filled with Love
- Obedience
- Total Submission
- Repentance

Praise Pretzels

What You Need
pretzel sticks
fondue pot with melted chocolate
wax paper

What to Do
1. Place the pretzels on the wax paper to form the word "praise."
2. Pick up the pretzels, one at a time, and dip the ends in melted chocolate (any end that must connect to another to form the letters).
3. Connect the pretzels to form each letter, then let the chocolate set firmly.
4. Enjoy the snack, or carry it home in a plastic bag. Make extras to share with others!

Praisins Snack

What You Need
1 cup raisins
¼ cup sugar
1 tablespoon cinnamon
plastic sandwich bags

What to Do
Place all the ingredients in a plastic bag and shake it until the raisins are coated.

Favorite Praise Popovers

What You Need
pie crust
favorite canned pie filling
powdered sugar

What to Do
1. Cut the pie crust dough into circles about the size of a saucer.
2. Place two tablespoons of your favorite filling in the center of the piecrust circle.
3. Fold the piecrust circle in half and pinch the edges together so the filling will not leak during baking.
4. Have an adult bake the popover in a 350°F oven or a toaster oven until the crust is golden brown.
5. Have an adult carefully remove the popover from the oven.
6. Sprinkle the popover with powdered sugar.
7. Allow to cool before eating.

Pop-up Praises

What You Need
Bag of microwave popcorn

What to Do
1. Place the bag of popcorn inside the microwave oven.
2. Listen carefully. Every time you hear a pop, name something for which you praise God. Think quickly, as you'll hear a lot of popping sounds!
3. Let the bag cool before you open it. While you enjoy your popcorn, think of some words to describe how you feel about God (love, admire, trust, etc.).

72

Notes of Praise

Psalm 18:3

I call to the **Lord**, who is worthy of **praise**.

bulletin board

WHAT YOU NEED
- duplicated page
- transparency sheets
- scissors
- permanent markers
- fishing line
- tape

WHAT TO DO
1. Duplicate the pattern page on a transparency sheet for each student.
2. Have the students cut the music notes from the transparency sheets.
3. Let the students use permanent markers to decorate the notes.
4. Have the students help you tie fishing line to hang the music notes throughout the room.
5. Say, **Many of the Psalms are like beautiful poems or songs. These notes will remind us that our awesome God is worthy of our praise.**

praise

CHAPTER 8

God Gives Unconditional Love

MEMORY VERSE

Know therefore that the Lord your God is God; he is the faithful God, keeping his covenant of love to a thousand generations of those who love him and keep his commands. DEUTERONOMY 7:9

✳ His Enduring Love ✳

In the book of Deuteronomy, God gives commands for His people. He was preparing His people to enter the Promised Land after He had led them out of slavery in Egypt. So He repeats the Ten Commandments, and He gives other instructions for how His people should live as a nation.

God told His people that they shouldn't fear the other nations around them. Even though those nations appeared stronger, God said He would help His people take the land from them. God always helps His followers.

In Deuteronomy 7, God says that He chose His people from all the people on the earth. God didn't choose them because they were good-looking or strong or large in number. He chose them because He loved them. God chooses His followers because He loves us.

God wasn't only saying those things for His people in those days. He meant them for us, too. He wants us to know that we have nothing to fear, no reason to worry, nothing to grumble about. We have something more precious than anything—we have the unconditional love of our Lord, the Almighty God!

BASED ON DEUTERONOMY 7

Discussion Questions

1. Why did God need to remind His followers about His rules?
2. How does it make you feel to know that God chose and loves you?

Love Given and Returned

How We Can Show Our Love to God

WHAT YOU NEED

- pages 76 and 77, duplicated
- construction paper
- scissors
- glue

WHAT TO DO

1. Before class, cut the phrases from the two pattern pages. Cut 23 large heart shapes from various colors of construction paper. Glue each phrase strip onto a separate heart shape. Hide the hearts around the room.
2. Begin the lesson by having the students read Deuteronomy 7:9 aloud together.
3. Say, **This chapter in Deuteronomy is just one example that tells of God's love for us and how we can show our love to Him. Love goes both ways. God freely gives us His love, and He wants us to love Him back.**
4. Have the students search for the 23 hearts. ➤

Make no treaty with them (enemies).
Break down altars, smash sacred stones, burn idols.
Love Him and keep His commands.
Take care to follow the commands, decrees, and laws God gave.
Pay attention to the laws and be careful to follow them.
Do not serve gods of the people you are to defeat for God.
Do not be afraid.
Do not be terrified of enemies.
Destroy idols and images of other gods.
Do not covet silver and gold of idols.

WHAT TO DO, CONTINUED

➤ 5. When all hearts have been found, say, **Some of the phrases on the hearts tell us about God's love for us. Others tell us how God's people should show love to Him. Work together to separate the two kinds of phrases, making two piles of the hearts.**
6. Have the students take turns reading aloud the phrases from the two heart piles by reading the ways God shows His love to us followed by the ways God's people can show love to God.
7. Have the students fasten the hearts to the bulletin board so they will be reminded of God's love for us and of how we can show our love for God.

How God Shows His Love for Us

The Lord your God brings you into the land you are entering to possess.
The Lord has delivered them (enemies) over to you.
You are a people holy to the Lord your God.
The Lord your God has chosen you out of all the people on the earth.
You are God's treasured possession.
God chose you because he loved you.
The Lord your God is faithful.
God keeps his covenant of love to a thousand generations.
God will keep his covenant of love.
God will love you and bless you, your children, your crops, your grain, your herds.
You will be blessed more than any other people.
Your God is a great and awesome God.
No one will be able to stand up against you.

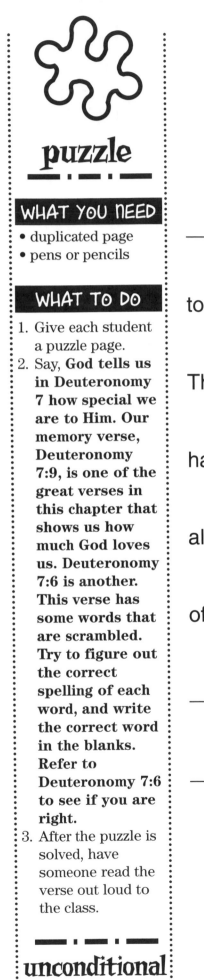

puzzle

WHAT TO DO

1. Give each student a puzzle page.
2. Say, **God tells us in Deuteronomy 7 how special we are to Him. Our memory verse, Deuteronomy 7:9, is one of the great verses in this chapter that shows us how much God loves us. Deuteronomy 7:6 is another. This verse has some words that are scrambled. Try to figure out the correct spelling of each word, and write the correct word in the blanks. Refer to Deuteronomy 7:6 to see if you are right.**
3. After the puzzle is solved, have someone read the verse out loud to the class.

unconditional

Scramble-back Words from God

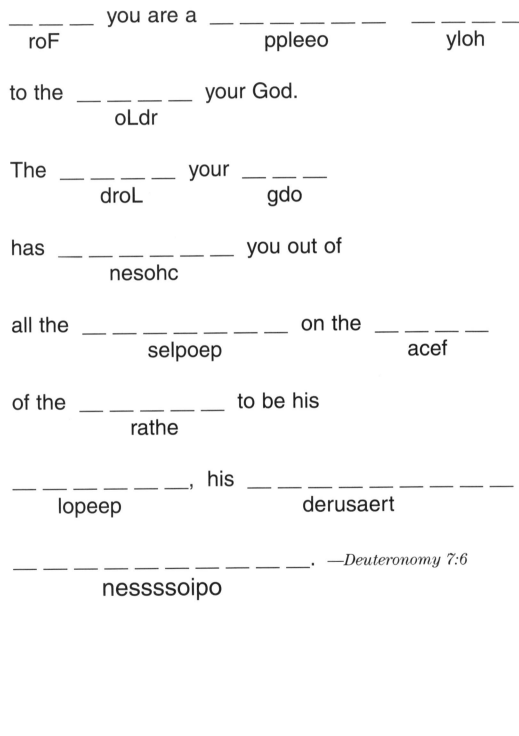

____ ___ you are a _____ ____
roF   ppleeo   yloh

to the ____ your God.
oLdr

The ____ your ___
droL   gdo

has _____ you out of
nesohc

all the _____ on the ____
selpoep   acef

of the _____ to be his
rathe

_____, his _____
lopeep   derusaert

_____. —*Deuteronomy 7:6*
nessssoipo

* Scrapbooking * My Family

Me

My Name is _____

Here is a picture of me

I was born on

_____ at

_____

Here are some important things about me:

_____

_____

_____

_____

_____

Know therefore that the Lord our God is God; he is the faithful God, keeping his covenant of love to a thousand generations of those who love him and keep his commands.

—Deuteronomy 7:9

WHAT YOU NEED

- this page and page 80, duplicated
- card stock
- wide clear adhesive tape
- markers
- pens
- scissors

WHAT TO DO

1. Before class, duplicate the pages to card stock for each student. Make several copies per student.
2. Say, **God tells us in our memory verse that He is the faithful God who keeps His covenant of love to all generations of those who love Him and keep His commands. A generation is the time between you and your parents, and so on. Your parents are one generation, your grandparents are another, etc. God promises to keep His covenant promise of love through all generations.**

WHAT TO DO, CONTINUED

3. Show how to use tape to bind the book together. First, stack all the pages together, keeping them even at the left edge. Carefully place the tape along the left edge, so that half of the width sticks to the front and half to the back of the closed book. Then open each page of the book, one at a time, and place a length of tape from top to bottom at the seam. Repeat with all the pages until the book is securely bound with the tape.
4. Let the students use pens or markers to fill in their scrapbooks. Say, **Fill in the first page to tell about yourself. When you get home, attach a picture of yourself to that page. Then use a separate page to write about each of your parents, grandparents, and all the relatives you can remember.**
5. Remind the students that God intended for His love to reach through all generations to the end of the world.

unconditional

About My Family

Name _____

Relationship to me _____

Birth date and place _____

What do I know about this person? _____

Attach a photo of a family member here

* The Lord Is * God Mobile

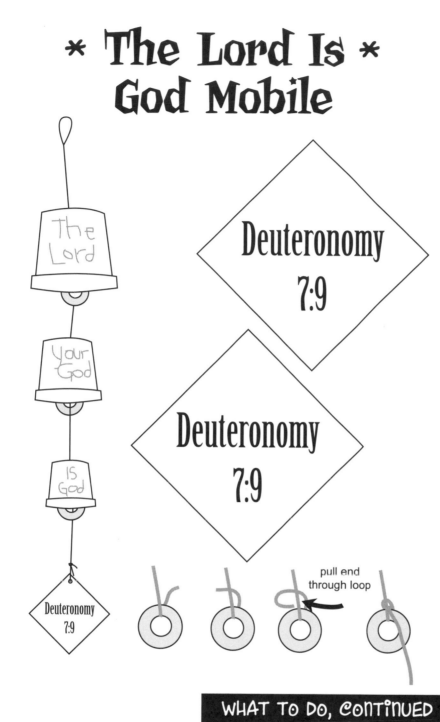

The Lord

Your God

Is God

Deuteronomy
7:9

Deuteronomy
7:9

Deuteronomy
7:9

pull end
through loop

WHAT TO DO, CONTINUED

➤ Allow the paint to dry, then spray the pots with clear acrylic so they can be hung outdoors.

4. Cut a one-yard length of plastic lacing for each student. Show how to thread the lacing through the holes in all three pots (largest pot on top; smallest on bottom), leaving a few inches of lacing above the top pot to form a loop for a hanger.

5. Show how to tie a washer inside the hole of each pot with the plastic lacing to hold the pot just so it overlaps the next one under it about an inch. Fasten the loose end of the loop at the top of the top pot by tying it to the washer just inside the pot.

6. Have each student use the remainder of the lacing length to hang below the smallest pot, and tape the laminated verse tag to the lacing.

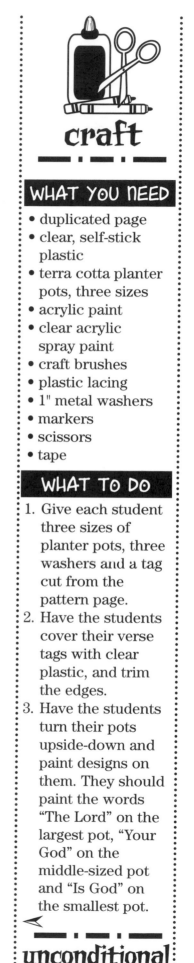

craft

WHAT YOU NEED

- duplicated page
- clear, self-stick plastic
- terra cotta planter pots, three sizes
- acrylic paint
- clear acrylic spray paint
- craft brushes
- plastic lacing
- 1" metal washers
- markers
- scissors
- tape

WHAT TO DO

1. Give each student three sizes of planter pots, three washers and a tag cut from the pattern page.
2. Have the students cover their verse tags with clear plastic, and trim the edges.
3. Have the students turn their pots upside-down and paint designs on them. They should paint the words "The Lord" on the largest pot, "Your God" on the middle-sized pot and "Is God" on the smallest pot.

➤

unconditional

group

WHAT YOU NEED

• duplicated page

WHAT TO DO

1. Use the ideas to the right to start discussions about the lesson from Deuteronomy 7.
2. Give each student an opportunity to participate in the discussion.
3. Listen carefully to what the students are saying, but try to let them do most of the discussion. Find the right moment to have the students pray for help in following God's commands and in solving any problems they have introduced.

unconditional

⁕ Discussion Starters ⁕

Q: God promises to drive out the ungodly from the Promised Land so His people could live there. How does that apply to us today?

Suggestions:
• God can drive away the enemies that would keep us from Him or from church.
• God can make us strong when we need to stand up for Christianity.
• God can be our protector during times of unrest in the world.

Q: God says people should not marry those from ungodly cities and lands. How does that apply to our relationships and marriages today?

Suggestions:
• God wants us to marry Christians so we have partners who encourage us to follow Him.
• God wants us to prayerfully consider those whom we might want to date.

Q: If we pay attention to God's laws and are careful to follow them, God will bless us more than any other people. Name some blessings you have that a non-believer wouldn't have.

Q: God says that He will repay with destruction those who do not love Him. Do you think He punishes us for our wrongdoing?

Suggestions:
• God sent Jesus to atone for our sins.
• We can repent and be forgiven.
• There are evil people in the world who hate God and God's people.

Q: God mentions many times in these verses that we are to follow His law and keep His commands. Name some of God's commandments.

Q: God tells His people not to be afraid of enemies, but to remember what they saw Him do in Egypt to free the Israelites from slavery. What have you witnessed God doing that helps you trust that He can and will take care of you?

Q: God tells people not to take images (idols) into their homes, and not to want any idols. What are some idols we might have today?

Suggestions:
• Money, selfishness, celebrities, things that keep us from God and from church.

* Covenant Lockets *

The Lord your God is God

The Lord your God is God

The Lord your God is God

The Lord your God is God

The Lord your God is God

WHAT YOU NEED

- duplicated page
- plastic soda bottle caps
- glue
- scissors
- gold or silver cord

WHAT TO DO

1. Give each student a duplicated page. Have the students cut out the verse circles from the page (they can make several lockets to share with others).
2. Have the students glue the verse circles inside the caps.
3. Each student should cut a 3-foot length of cord and fold it in half.
4. Show how to spread glue around the outside of the cap and wrap the cord around the cap, centering the cord so an even length is left over on both sides.
5. The students should tie the loose ends of the cords together.

WHAT TO DO, CONTINUED

➤ 6. Tell the students they can use the lockets for necklaces or key chains, or hang them in their rooms to remember God's covenant of love throughout the generations.

unconditional

puzzle

WHAT YOU NEED

- duplicated page
- pens or pencils

WHAT TO DO

1. Give each student a puzzle page.
2. Have the students read the memory verse out loud.
3. Say, **The memory verse says our God has promised His love to us, and He will be faithful to show that love to a thousand generations. The word "love" appears many times in the word search puzzle. Circle all of them. How many did you find?**

unconditional

* Fifty Times Love *

```
L O V E E V O L O L O V E E V O L
O O M E X X X O O Z Q E V O L
V E V O L R T V P V T L V L O
E O G E E D L E L K E O O F V
L C B V T L O V E R W V N M E
G R O O G L O V E L E E O N L
F L B L W Q E P R L O V E L O
T E V O L O V E H G O V O C V
I L O V E L X V D S Q V E E E
L Y T E E O L O V E E B E V L
O U U V X V R L R V B V Q O O
V L B O T E O R O X E V O L V
E V O L W V U L X V E V O L E
N O W V P O R L O V E V O L S
T L O V E L L O V E V O L Q P
```

CHAPTER 9

More Awesome God Activities

God's the most awesome thing that ever could be.
Just look how happy He has made me.
God is the most awesome one I know.
I love Him and He loves me so.

Awesome, awesome, my God is awesome to me, to me.
Awesome, awesome, what a wonderful God is He.

God takes care of me every day.
He guides me all along my way.
God delights in showing me His love.
I sing praises to my God above.

Chorus

God wants me to live in His ways.
To follow His laws all my days.
God promises to bless me and keep me,
If a faithful child of His I will be.

Chorus

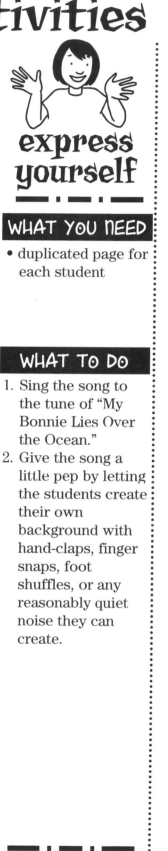

express yourself

WHAT YOU NEED

• duplicated page for each student

WHAT TO DO

1. Sing the song to the tune of "My Bonnie Lies Over the Ocean."
2. Give the song a little pep by letting the students create their own background with hand-claps, finger snaps, foot shuffles, or any reasonably quiet noise they can create.

more!

* Clip Art Pages *

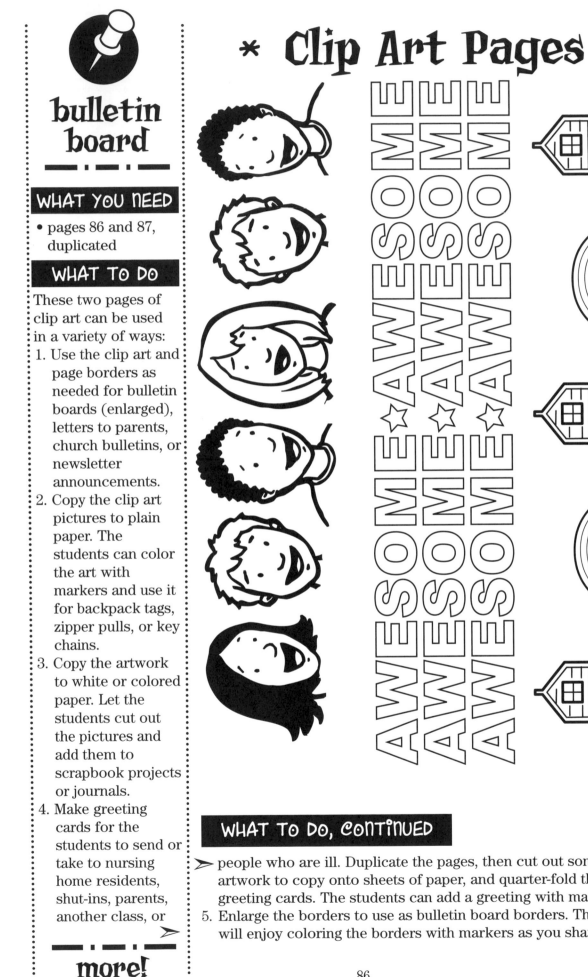

bulletin board

WHAT YOU NEED
- pages 86 and 87, duplicated

WHAT TO DO

These two pages of clip art can be used in a variety of ways:

1. Use the clip art and page borders as needed for bulletin boards (enlarged), letters to parents, church bulletins, or newsletter announcements.

2. Copy the clip art pictures to plain paper. The students can color the art with markers and use it for backpack tags, zipper pulls, or key chains.

3. Copy the artwork to white or colored paper. Let the students cut out the pictures and add them to scrapbook projects or journals.

4. Make greeting cards for the students to send or take to nursing home residents, shut-ins, parents, another class, or

more!

WHAT TO DO, CONTINUED

➤ people who are ill. Duplicate the pages, then cut out some of the artwork to copy onto sheets of paper, and quarter-fold them into greeting cards. The students can add a greeting with markers.

5. Enlarge the borders to use as bulletin board borders. The students will enjoy coloring the borders with markers as you share lessons.

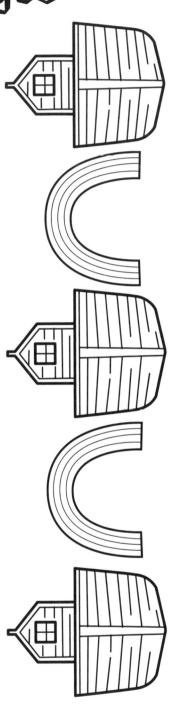

AWESOME

COVENANT

LORD GOD

group

* Awesome *
Scripture Search

Exodus 15:11

Exodus 34:10

Deuteronomy 4:34

Deuteronomy 7:21

Deuteronomy 10:17

Deuteronomy 10:21

2 Samuel 7:23

1 Chronicles 17:21

Nehemiah 1:5

Nehemiah 4:14

Job 37:22

Psalm 45:4

Psalm 47:2

Psalm 65:5

Psalm 66:3

Psalm 66:5

Psalm 68:35

Psalm 89:7

Psalm 99:3

Psalm 111:9

Psalm 145:6

Isaiah 64:3

Daniel 9:4

Take the Challenge!

- [ ] Exodus 15:1-18 –
  Song of Moses and Miriam after escape from Egypt

- [ ] Exodus 23:10-13 – Laws of Justice and Mercy

- [ ] Isaiah 9:1-7 – Promise of a Savior

- [ ] Psalm 63 – Praise

- [ ] Psalm 92 – Praise

- [ ] Psalm 93 – Praise

- [ ] Psalm 100 – Praise

- [ ] Psalm 150 – Praise

- [ ] Proverbs 3:1-6 – Benefits of Wisdom

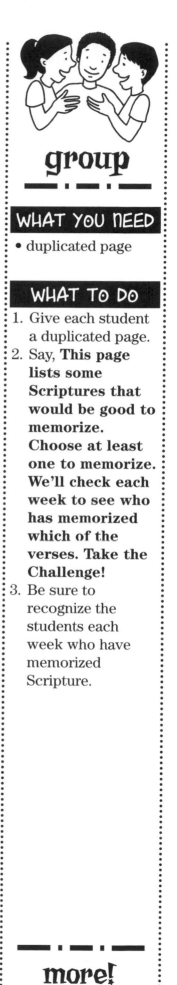

group

WHAT YOU NEED
- duplicated page

WHAT TO DO
1. Give each student a duplicated page.
2. Say, **This page lists some Scriptures that would be good to memorize. Choose at least one to memorize. We'll check each week to see who has memorized which of the verses. Take the Challenge!**
3. Be sure to recognize the students each week who have memorized Scripture.

more!

bulletin board

WHAT YOU NEED

- pages 90 and 91, duplicated
- 12" x 12" corkboards
- craft foam
- glue
- scissors
- glue gun
- acrylic paint
- craft paintbrushes
- pencils

WHAT TO DO

1. Give each student a duplicated page and a 12" x 12" corkboard.
2. Have the students cut out the designs they want to use from the pattern pages.
3. They should trace the shapes onto craft foam and cut them out.
4. Have each student cut four 11" strips from the craft foam. They can cut the strips with decorative edges, such as scalloped, if they want.
5. Have the students glue the strips along the edges of their corkboards.

more!

* Awesome God *
Bulletin Board

WHAT TO DO, CONTINUED

6. Help the students use a glue gun to attach their foam shapes to the boards.
7. Have the students write "Awesome God" in the centers of their corkboards, and then paint the letters.

91

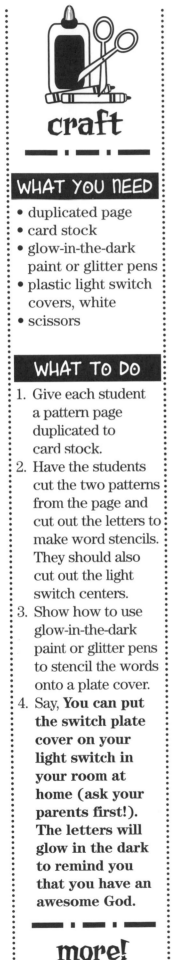

craft

WHAT YOU NEED

- duplicated page
- card stock
- glow-in-the-dark paint or glitter pens
- plastic light switch covers, white
- scissors

WHAT TO DO

1. Give each student a pattern page duplicated to card stock.
2. Have the students cut the two patterns from the page and cut out the letters to make word stencils. They should also cut out the light switch centers.
3. Show how to use glow-in-the-dark paint or glitter pens to stencil the words onto a plate cover.
4. Say, **You can put the switch plate cover on your light switch in your room at home (ask your parents first!). The letters will glow in the dark to remind you that you have an awesome God.**

more!

✳ Glow in the Dark ✳ Light Switch Cover

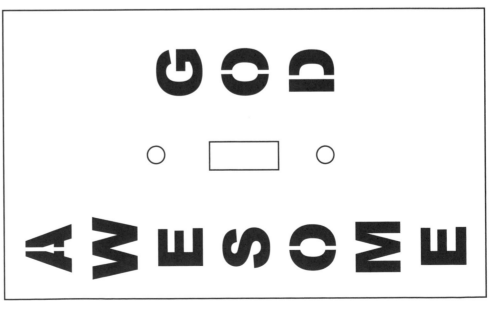

✴ Praise Words Game ✴

PRAISE WORDS:

AWESOME

GREAT

ALMIGHTY

LORD

CREATOR

ONE GOD

MAJESTY

PRAISE

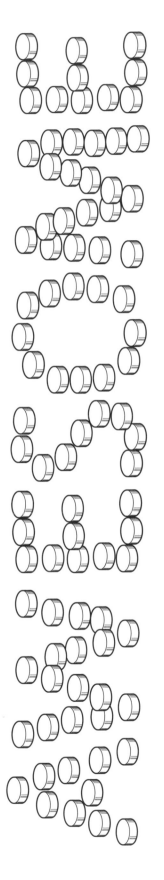

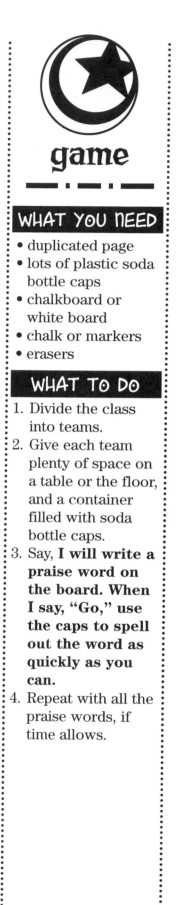

game

WHAT YOU NEED

- duplicated page
- lots of plastic soda bottle caps
- chalkboard or white board
- chalk or markers
- erasers

WHAT TO DO

1. Divide the class into teams.
2. Give each team plenty of space on a table or the floor, and a container filled with soda bottle caps.
3. Say, **I will write a praise word on the board. When I say, "Go," use the caps to spell out the word as quickly as you can.**
4. Repeat with all the praise words, if time allows.

more!

Our Awesome God Answer Key

Page 8: The Four P's
Grieved; Righteous; Blameless; Walked

Page 11: Search the Word
Created: 5; Made: 5; Said: 11; Called: 4; Blessed: 2

Page 12: Befuddled Blueprints
Project 1: table
Project 2: beanbag chair

Page 22: Wilderness Team
Egypt; God's plan; Red Sea; none; a pillar of cloud; a pillar of fire; grumbled; it was sour; a piece of wood; quail; manna; water came from a rock

Page 30: Double Puzzle
Puzzle 1: Take off your sandals, for the place where you stand is holy.
Puzzle 2: Reverence

Page 40: The King Learns a Lesson

```
J R (Z I T H E R) B   E D (S T O
(G O V E R N O R S) N T (E Q R
V N (H) G P F G R S   N I T R O
(R (S A T R A P S) N  Z Z A L K
I O (R O B E S) S E   T P R U N
A N (P I P E S) X B   M B T L I
(H) O R (N) E S (E T U L F) S M N
Q (J U D G E S) A C   A M I F R
J U D B N M O H H   H V G O (M
T (S R E S I V D A) U Y A H E
P L U (A) M B X I D   D O (M) C S
(B) B E (B) E D R O N  U P Q A H
(O (T R E A S U R E R S) A R A
D O O D O O R A Z   A B B D C
I U O N E B A A Z   A R Q A H
E E E E R U N S A   B R O H H
S G O G N O (L Y R E) N O S E
J E S (O (P R E F E C T) S R G
```

Our Awesome God Answer Key

Page 48: Flip Flop Bible Search

66; 2; Matthew; In the beginning; Amen; they are God-breathed; Matthew, Mark, Luke and John; 150; Malachi; "Songs" or "Solomon"; John; 4; Proverbs; Revelation; Numbers; Isaiah; John's and Jesus'; That you might believe that Jesus is the Christ, the Son of God; Read and hear God's Word; The Lord's love; Jesus; Remember me with favor, O my God.

Page 58: God Gives a Promise
"For I will forgive their wickedness and will remember their sins no more."
—Jeremiah 31:34

Page 64: It Bears Repeating
Psalm 18:1-3 — 2 Samuel 22:2-4
Psalm 96:4 — Psalm 145:3
Psalm 48:1 — 1 Chronicles 16:25
Psalm 18:49 — 2 Samuel 22:50
Psalm 103:1 — Psalm 146:1
1 Kings 8:15 — 2 Chronicles 6:4

Page 78: Scramble-back Words from God
"For you are a people holy to the Lord your God. The Lord your God has chosen you out of all the peoples on the face of the earth to be his people, his treasured possession." —Deuteronomy 7:6

Page 84: Fifty Times Love
"Love" appears fifty times in the word search.